UNLOCKING THE DREAM

THE ULTIMATE DREAM INTERPRETATION GUIDE

SYLVESTER RANKINE, MA

Unlocking the Dream: The Ultimate Dream Interpretation Guide
Trilogy Christian Publishers A Wholly Owned Subsidiary of Trinity Broadcasting Network
2442 Michelle Drive, Tustin, CA 92780
Copyright © 2022 by Sylvester Rankine
Scripture quotations marked NIV are taken from the Holy Bible, New International Version®, NIV®. Copyright © 1973, 1978, 1984, 2011 by Biblica, Inc.TM Used by permission of Zondervan. All rights reserved worldwide. www.zondervan.com. The "NIV" and "New International Version" are trademarks registered in the United States Patent and Trademark Office by Biblica, Inc.TM Scripture quotations marked NKJV are taken from the New King James Version®. Copyright © 1982 by Thomas Nelson. Used by permission. All rights reserved. Scripture quotations marked KJV are taken from the King James Version of the Bible. Public domain.
No part of this book may be reproduced, stored in a retrieval system, or transmitted by any means without written permission from the author. All rights reserved. Printed in the USA.
Rights Department, 2442 Michelle Drive, Tustin, CA 92780.
Trilogy Christian Publishing/TBN and colophon are trademarks of Trinity Broadcasting Network.
Cover design by: Trilogy
For information about special discounts for bulk purchases, please contact Trilogy Christian Publishing.
Trilogy Disclaimer: The views and content expressed in this book are those of the author and may not necessarily reflect the views and doctrine of Trilogy Christian Publishing or the Trinity Broadcasting Network.
Manufactured in the United States of America
10 9 8 7 6 5 4 3 2 1
Library of Congress Cataloging-in-Publication Data is available.
ISBN: 978-1-68556-933-4
E-ISBN: 978-1-68556-934-1

DEDICATION

This book is dedicated to my children, Joel, Janae, and Josh-Daniel. I love you dearly.

Acknowledgments

To my Lord and Savior, Jesus Christ, thank You for entrusting me to deliver this great treasure to Your people and for giving me my spiritual mentors, Pastor Alberta Miller and Pastor Ermine Phillip. Thank You for your unwavering commitment to my success.

My incredible wife, Nyala Williams-Rankine, for your love and support, I will forever honor and cherish you, darling.

I am eternally grateful for my loving and supportive family, Joseph and Ruby Rankine, Verna Williams, Marvalyn, Schoma, Andre, Nekeya, Carmelo, Shelly, Maxine, Shanielle, Shamaine, Castell, Daniel, Winston, Nathan, Sylvan, Jamaine and Anthonile. You are my strength and inspiration.

All my students, whom I have learned a whole lot from during our dream class journey. You have certainly made the teaching-learning experiences most meaningful.

Thanks to my Citadel Family as well as all my global supporters and ministry partners. Thank you for believing in me.

Finally, there can never be a great book without an even greater publisher. Thank you, TBN Trilogy Christian Publishing, for doing an exceptional job. May God forever favor and bless your invaluable and inspirational team.

TABLE OF CONTENTS

Acknowledgments................................V

Introduction....................................IX

Chapter 1: Our Dreamworld........................1

Chapter 2: Tips for Dream Interpretation..........11

Chapter 3: Number Symbolism.....................21

Chapter 4: Color Symbolism......................37

Chapter 5: Imagery & Symbols....................45

Chapter 6: Animals..............................59

Chapter 7: Birds................................93

Chapter 8: Insects & Reptiles...................107

Chapter 9: Human Anatomy & Physiology..........119

Chapter 10: Elements of the Waters..............165

Chapter 11: Final Unlocking (A-Z)...............175

Chapter 12: Powerful Warfare Prayers............193

Conclusion.....................................211

Appendix.......................................215

Bibliography...................................233

Introduction

Dr. Martin Luther King Jr.'s most captivating and valuable phrase was, "I have a dream." Even though his dream surrounded his philosophical ideas as opposed to getting instructions while being asleep, it still galvanized his spirit and propelled his cause for change. Even today, his phrase, "I have a dream," still lives on and inspires many. That's how powerful a dream is!

If you haven't been dreaming, you may need to start now. Ask Almighty God to release the anointing of a dreamer upon you. Whether we hold the office of a prophet or not, all of us need God's divine instructions and revelations, now more than ever. This is available through our dreams. As we gear down towards the end time dispensation, God is revealing Himself and His kingdom assignments to His people through dreams in even greater proportions.

Are you making the most of your dream? Are you taking advantage of the *opportunity* each dream is pregnant with? Make a conscious effort to move from being in the unknown to the known. Let today be the day when you pay greater attention to the message that your dream is sending. Dreams offer great insights and revelations that, if properly interpreted, can place us ahead of the game.

Employing the right interpretation skills is like using an excellent GPS that allows us to traverse the terrains of life. In other words, our dreams are very important and must be interpreted within the right context, as each dream may have multiple meanings. We must examine our dreams' contents, frequencies, and the emotions they stir within us in order to decode their hidden gems.

If you ever dream or someone tells you about their dream, and you struggle to interpret it, this book is definitely for you. I am so convinced that this power-packed book will transform your life and pivot you into a place of dominion. In *Unlocking the Dream*, you will discover at least twelve keys to how to accurately interpret your dreams. I will walk you through step by step how to interpret dreams concerning numbers, colors, insects, reptiles, animals, and humans, and the list continues. Without a doubt, you will master the art of dream interpretation. In addition, you will also be empowered to know exactly what to do after you unlock the dream. This book is loaded with examples of both the most common and unfamiliar dreams. Furthermore, in *Unlocking the Dream*, prayers are strategically tailored to meet each dream's scenarios, thus equipping the reader to obtain greater awareness of when and how to pray against diabolical disturbances seen in their dreams.

Having said all this, perfecting the art of unlocking our dreams also requires us to humbly rely on the Creator for insights. The same God who gave "Joseph—the dreamer" the divine skills and authority to competently unlock dreams is still activating this gift today. We don't need to turn to any sorcery or psychic powers when we have the Holy Spirit, who happens to be the greatest teacher and revealer of all hidden mysteries. Let's get connected to

Introduction

God today! Great treasures await us. It's time to unlock the dream!

CHAPTER 1:
OUR DREAMWORLD

"Dreams are channels through which people receive warnings, divine instructions, and guidance from Almighty God."

In the year 2020, a tragic life-threatening situation occurred. After going for a regular evening jog, I was tirelessly walking home when suddenly two men dressed in black hoodies alighted from a black SUV and said, "Don't move!" I was immediately frozen. They quickly grabbed me and attempted to put me inside the vehicle. Somehow, miraculously, I mustered the strength, struggled free from my attackers, and dashed into a nearby trail with the men heavily pursuing me. Not even the Tokyo 2021 Olympic one-hundred-meter finals combination speed of the Jamaican trio, Elaine Thompson-Herah (10.61), Shelly Ann-Fraser Pryce (10.74), and Shericka Jackson (10.76), could have caught me. I ran breathlessly, with my heart pounding and my feet aching, only to realize later that I was only dreaming!

The encounter felt so real; it gripped me for days and even affected my sleep pattern. Interestingly, many people are experiencing similar dreams of this nature—being chased by men, animals, insects, and the list goes on. There is absolutely no doubt that the attacker or the pursuer's intention is to kill, steal, and destroy. These dreams often feel so real! Like a stone thrown in a body of calm water that causes a transverse wave to occur, dreams of this nature often make the dreamer experience a ripple effect in their emotional and psychological state.

To many, dreams are fascinating "night movies" of the mind. Notwithstanding, no one likes having dreams of being chased or bitten. No one looks forward to dreams involving falling from a height of 42,000 feet, like a commercial plane, or falling perpetually and somehow unable to reach the ground. These dreams are often horrific and are sometimes very challenging to wake up from. At the same time, impacting the individual's emotional and psychological state for days. Not surprisingly, dreamers rather prefer to experience only pleasurable dreams, those that involve picking ripe fruits or being given lots of money. Nevertheless, whether pleasant or unpleasant, our dreams offer revelations of our past, present, and future. To be more specific, our dreams are like miniature films that reveal to us what took place in our past, what is currently happening, or what is likely to take place in our tomorrow.

Chapter 1: Our Dreamworld

Sadly, many dreams are often misunderstood, misinterpreted, or even ignored because they seem foolish or just don't make sense. A word of caution, though, don't be fooled! Our dreams are very important, and those who know how to effectively interpret them will benefit tremendously by doing so. Importantly, one of the primary ways through which God communicates to His people is through dreams. As a matter of fact, there are numerous references in the Bible through which God sends messages to persons of all categories through dreams. A few of these persons include Joseph (Genesis 37:9–11), Daniel (Daniel 2:1–16), Solomon (2 Chronicles 1:7), and Nebuchadnezzar (Daniel 10:1–14).

Notably, during the time of the birth of Jesus, His earthly father, Joseph, was given insightful instructions in his dreams by angelic visitation. Joseph understood the importance of dreams, like many others in his time, and thus was able to unlock the dream. How did Joseph benefit? He gained great insights and was able to follow God's instruction, which led to the supernatural protection of baby Jesus from impending harm and danger (Matthew 2). Can you imagine if Joseph had not understood or ignored his dream? What a tragedy that would have been.

Like in the golden days of old, God is still using dreams today to give a burst of both natural and spiritual revelations to His people. The Book of Joel captures it by emphasizing that in the last days or during the end time dispensation, God will pour out His Spirit upon all flesh. By what means is this pouring out going to take place?

Through dreams, visions, and prophecies (Joel 2:28–29).

Whether young or old, rich or poor, beyond gender barriers, racial or religious discriminations, God is revealing great insights about His kingdom to His people like never before! In light of this, even if we are not dream experts, it is still imperative in this end-time era to learn at least some basic dream interpretation skills. Knowing how to interpret our dreams and those of our loved ones will definitely equip us to rule from a place of victory and authority.

DEFINITION OF DREAM

What is a dream? A dream refers to the "subjective conscious experiences occurring during sleep" (Sikka et al., 2018). It is "a series of thoughts, images, or emotions occurring during sleep" (Merriam-Webster, 2022). One of the Hebrew words used for "dream" is *Chalom*, and it refers to "ordinary dreams of sleep; prophetic dreams and revelations." In contrast, two Greek words used for dreams are *Enupnion* and *Onar*, which mean "something seen in sleep" as well as "a vision in sleep, in distinction from waking vision," respectively (Strong, 2001). This is key as many people often misunderstand the difference between dreams and visions. The most prominent difference is that dreams occur while we are asleep as opposed to visions that occur while we are awake.

Chapter 1: Our Dreamworld

CATEGORIES OF DREAMS

With this said, dreams normally fall into three main categories, namely:

1. *Divine or Spiritual Dreams*: These dreams are those that are inspired by the Almighty God. They are distinctive because they generally offer special instructions. Divine dreams are frequently given to guide people from imminent harm or danger. God also uses these dreams to significantly bless His people (1 Kings 3:5–15; Matthew 2:13).

2. *Diabolical or Demonic Dreams*: As the name suggests, these dreams are inspired by Satan and his wicked cohorts. When people are spiritually attacked in their dreams, it is a sign that diabolic attacks are actively set in motion. They are the ones that paralyze the dreamer with fears and anxieties. These dreams are geared toward interrupting and destroying people's lives and destinies. From deception to disasters, diabolic dreams are the ones that infringe upon the dreamer. As a matter of fact, many individuals have reported even being raped or sexually abused by occultists and Dark Arts practitioners who astral project in their dream world (please see my book entitled *Kill That Dog: Deliverance from the Dog Spirit*).

3. *Natural or Soulful Dreams*: These dreams are those inspired by the natural processes of a person's mind, will, and emotions. For example, the person may have been meditating on a

particular thing throughout the day and later finds themselves having a dream about the same issue because the dreamer's mind, will, or emotion earnestly desires the thing to happen.

In light of all this, correctly assessing the source of our dreams becomes important in order for us to know which category of dream we are currently experiencing. Therefore, discernment is the key to determining or unlocking the source of our dream. We must examine each dream within its context while seeking God earnestly through prayers for revelation.

THE IMPORTANCE OF OUR DREAMS

Firstly, dreams are channels that God uses to supernaturally bless His people. No matter how incredulous it sounds, God actually visits and blesses His people even while they are sleeping. Countless individuals have received cutting-edge concepts, witty inventions, business ideas, ideas on how to write books, compose songs, and so on, through dreams. Therefore, by unlocking their dreams, many people have received great insights and revelations that propel them to be the best in their industries.

In 2 Chronicles 1:7–12 and 1 Kings 3:5–28, God visited Solomon in his dream and revolutionized his life with a mind-blowing opportunity that made him earn the title of the wisest and richest king during his lifetime.

Chapter 1: Our Dreamworld

In his dream encounter, Solomon was told by God, "Ask for whatever you want Me to give you." Solomon's response was critical as it would set the stage for what was to next unfold. Solomon said, "Give me wisdom and knowledge so that I may lead Your people." His response pleased God so much that God not only gave him wisdom and knowledge but He also rewarded him with wealth, possessions, and honor, which was greater than any other king before and after him ever experienced. Do you see how powerful your dream is? One dream encounter can totally transform your life. I don't know about you, but I want God to visit me in my dream like Solomon and shower me with His golden goodies.

Secondly, dreams are not only used by God, but they are also channels the enemy uses to attack, harass, and torment people. Many people have been constantly bombarded by spiritual attacks in their dreams. They have received dreams, and shortly after, evil manifestations, such as sicknesses, deaths, accidents, financial deficits, breakthrough interruptions, and the list continues, occurred. The devil and his minions come to kill, steal, and destroy, and one way to carry out their vicious intent is by attacking individuals in their dreams.

Interestingly, this is how Job puts it,

> *A word was secretly brought to me, my ears caught a whisper of it. Amid disquieting dreams in the night when deep sleep falls on people. Fear and trembling seized me and made all my bones shake. A spirit glided*

> *past my face, and the hair on my body stood on end. It stopped, but I could not tell what it was. A form stood before my eyes, and I heard a hushed voice.*
>
> **Job 4:12–16 (NIV)**

Wow! What an encounter. No wonder the Bible says, "While men slept, his enemy came and sowed tares…" (Matthew 13:25, KJV). The enemy is always roaming, seeking whomever he can devour. Unfortunately, he is devouring a lot of people in their dreams.

Thirdly, dreams are channels through which people receive warnings, divine instructions, and guidance from the Almighty God. In Genesis 20:3, Abimelech was warned by God in his dream not to sleep with Abraham's wife or else he would die! Similarly, Pilate was warned by his wife not to interfere in the ruling of Jesus because of the dreams that she had received concerning him (Matthew 27:19). Then, in Matthew 2:13, 20–25, Joseph received divine instructions from God in his dream, which guided him in protecting baby Jesus from untimely or premature death. Still, the apostle Paul was also guided by his dreams and visions during his various missionary trips (Acts 16:6–10). All in all, in Genesis 41, Pharaoh had a dream that was carefully unlocked by Joseph to save a nation and its people from a devastating famine. As a matter of fact, Joseph's dream interpretation skills guided him to secure and design an award-winning preparation plan that made Pharaoh and his people conquer the famine.

In light of this, I cannot overemphasize that our dreams

Chapter 1: Our Dreamworld

are super important. In other words, our dreams must not be scantly ignored or disregarded. Our dreams need to be properly unlocked. They must be correctly interpreted, as by so doing, we will gain tremendous insights. Unlocking our dreams will allow us to seize every available hidden opportunity for great success. Like Joseph, who unlocked the dream and received promotions, was taken from the pit to the palace, and became second in command to the famous king, so too will we reap the benefits of interpretations of our dreams.

As mentioned before, proper unlocking of our dreams requires us to interpret them within the right context, as dreams can have multiple meanings. For example, doves normally symbolize "gentleness"; however, if you dreamt of a white dove attacking you, it definitely cannot be interpreted as "gentleness" or "peaceful." Here the key to unlocking this dream concerns what the bird was doing. It was attacking! Thus, we must exercise acuity like Solomon when we are unlocking our dreams.

CHAPTER 2:
TIPS FOR DREAM INTERPRETATION

"If you cannot immediately remember your dream, do not become overly anxious. Instead, just lay still, meditate, pray, worship, or ask the Holy Spirit to bring back the dream to you."

We have already established at least three reasons why our dreams are important. They are channels God uses to bless His people; they are also channels through which we receive sound warnings, and dreams are also channels the enemy uses to attack people. With this in mind, correctly interpreting our dreams allows us to superimpose the plan of God over and against the plans of the adversary. We are able to disrupt every evil assignment and, instead, call forth the manifestations of God's divine blessings at the correct timing.

Consequently, whether we are dreamers like Joseph or just so happen to get a dream once in a while like Pharaoh, one thing is fundamentally clear, we must have at least a basic understanding of how to unlock or interpret our dreams. By so doing, we will be able to operate from a place of dominion and clarity like the sons of Issachar, who understood correct times and seasons. Their wisdom promoted them above their counterparts as only they knew what the best course for Israel should have been (1 Chronicles 12:32).

KEY QUESTIONS TO ASK WHEN UNLOCKING OUR DREAMS:

1. How did the dream end? Were you victorious in the dream, or did your dream end in you suffering defeats?
2. Does the message of the dream reflect the character of Christ, or is it reflecting the nature of the devil?
3. Does the dream "line up" with the Word of God, or does it go against the teachings of the Bible?
4. Is the message of the dream self-serving, supports unholy desires, or does it advocate righteousness?

Like the Global Positioning System (GPS), asking and receiving answers to these questions will definitely position us in the right direction of unlocking the mysteries behind our dreams. Ultimately, this will always give us

Chapter 2: Tips for Dream Interpretation

the edge over the deceptive schemes of the enemy and hence make us victorious in our battles. Let us now look more closely at some dream interpretation tips that you will certainly find most helpful in unlocking your dreams and those of your loved ones.

TWELVE KEYS TO UNLOCKING OUR DREAMS

1. *Record It Immediately*: Immediately after waking up, write your dreams down or use a recording instrument such as your phone to record the details. Whether by using the Notepad app or the Voice Memos app. It doesn't matter once it is retrievable when you make a record of it. Why? Many times, people tend to forget their dreams when they are not recorded instantly. Immediately after waking up from the dream, the details or impressions are usually fresh in the mind of the dreamer, thus making it quite easier to secure the relevant information for its interpretation.

2. *Determine the Source*: This cannot be overemphasized. Here the purpose is to determine if you are being spiritually attacked, intruded on, or manipulated by the enemy or whether God is giving you revelations or instructions. Therefore, doing a thorough assessment or exercising discernment becomes very important to decipher what is happening. Notably, one of the greatest strategies used by the enemy concerning dreams is deception. Therefore, when interpreting the dream, you must align your dream with the Word of God to ascertain if it is God revealing or the

devil deceiving.

3. *Identify Feelings/Emotions*: How did you feel while having the dream? How did you feel immediately after or when you woke up from the dream? How did the people, animals, or birds appear in your dream? What emotions did the dream stir up? Were they feelings of excitement, sadness, happiness, anger, awe, fear, jubilation, or terror? Deciphering the emotions that the dream generates is also key to unraveling its mysteries. A dream that generates good emotions or feelings is normally a good dream. On the other hand, dreams that evoke feelings of fear, anxiety, anger, and other negative emotions must not be taken lightly. These dreams require urgent cancellation through prayer and other godly spiritual strategies.

4. *Severity/Intensity*: How severe was the encounter in the dream? On a scale of 1–10, with ten being the highest, representing most severe, and one being the lowest, representing least severe, where would you rank your feelings after having the dream encounter? Were you injured in the dream and woke up feeling intense pain? Were you crying because of being hurt and woke up seeing the actual marks or bruises on your body? Were you having sex in the dream and then woke up feeling the area penetrated or seeing the physical signs of when a person made love to their partner? (Example: seeing discharge or blood.) Here, intensity and severity become vital to decoding our dreams. Sadly, many individuals are still naive to think that it's just a dream even

Chapter 2: Tips for Dream Interpretation

when they see physical signs of the attack. No wonder the Bible says, "My people are destroyed for a lack of knowledge" (Hosea 4:6, NIV). The next time you receive a dream that evokes a particular emotion or causes physical marks on your body or other tell-tale signs, please take note and assess the severity. This will certainly help you to unlock the dream. Also, please take decisive actions to cancel and sever any demonic dream attacks through immediate declarations, prayer, and fasting.

5. *Determine the Frequencies*: How often do you get this type of dream? Very often, sometimes, once, every year, every month, every two weeks, every full moon? To decode our dreams, we must pay keen attention to frequency. Examining the frequencies of our dreams is very important as it reveals the nature or type as well as the severity, especially during spiritual warfare. Furthermore, by examining the frequencies of our dreams, we are able to determine if diabolic cycles, as well as evil strongholds, are in operation. Once a demonic cycle or evil stronghold is established in a person's life, the solution requires urgent active, forceful, persistent, and consistent prayers for breaking these evil cycles.

6. *Examine the Specific Time of Occurrence*: When did you receive the dream? Was it 6 a.m., 3 a.m., 12 p.m., every twilight, every full moon? Here again, time is very important, as it reveals essential patterns and indicates consistency or irregularity. Those who are skillful in spiritual warfare will explain that even though the enemy

is always active, like a roaring lion, there are specific times when the enemy may intensify his operation. For example, between the hours of 12 a.m.–3 a.m., midday and midnights. For those practicing evil arts, time is very important when launching their evil attacks. Therefore, to counter demonic attacks that are time-bound, we must become spiritually alert or time-sensitive. During spiritual warfare, the believer may need to establish patterns of praying. For example, ensure you are praying during the midnight hours when you normally receive a tormenting dream. Set your alarm to wake you up fifteen minutes before the dream attack is launched, and engage in strategic prayer and worship to interrupt the plan of the enemy. Activate the Word of God and legislate that, "The sun shall not smite thee by day, nor the moon by night" (Psalm 121:6, KJV).

7. *Study the Patterns*: Does the dream have a recurring theme, or is it just a one-off situation? Is it always a child, old person, animal, dirty or clean water, or sexual encounter dream? Here the dreamer must pay keen attention to patterns as these give great clues to unraveling the mystery of our dream. For example, a dream of dirty water is indicative of danger versus one of clear water. Notwithstanding, always remember to dissect your dream within context as the enemy is very deceptive. Here the Holy Spirit becomes very helpful as He is the revealer of all truth.

8. *Check the Sequence/Order*: How did the dream unfold? What happened first, second, third, and so on. How many people or animals attacked you

Chapter 2: Tips for Dream Interpretation

first? How did the dream end? If your dream ends in triumph, it is definitely a positive indicator that you have conquered your enemy or will be victorious. However, if your dream ends in you being defeated by the enemy, that's not a good dream. You must take it seriously; advance in serious prayer to cancel and sever the devices of the enemy! Without a doubt, checking the sequences or order of our dreams will enhance our dream interpretation skills.

9. *Number*: How many people, animals, birds, and insects were in the dream? How much money did you see in the dream? Numbers are key symbols to decode our dream as each number carries a particular meaning. Importantly, numbers can convey multiple meanings; hence, when we are dissecting our dreams, we must pay keen attention to context and connect the numbers to the other tips given rather than viewing them in isolation. For example, the number sixteen may mean something different in the occult world than it does in biblical interpretation, and still, the Hebrew interpretation may even carry another meaning. The key is to know if the number seen is working for you or working against you. By so doing, you will be able to know what action to take, that is, in other words, whether to nullify attacks or to superimpose the blessings. In keeping with this, I will give greater details in the upcoming chapters on numbers.

10. *Pay Attention to Style/Design*: What was the color of the bird, animal, or building? What were the people wearing? What was the color of the

water? What symbol was written on the paper or wall? When applying this tip, style or design offers great insight for interpreting our dreams. Like numbers, colors also carry significance and meaning, which must not be overlooked when interpreting our dreams. I will also examine these in greater detail as we journey into the subsequent chapters.

11. *Setting*: Where were you in the dream? Were you at a cemetery/graveyard, school, a church, on the road, or in a yard? Were you at the former community that you grew up in? Were you by a body of water (pond, lake, river, or sea)? Examining the place where you were in the dream is very important to unlock your dreams. Again, examining the setting of our dreams can point us to identify what spiritual forces are waging war against us. For example, many times, dreaming of former communities is connected to a spirit of regression or anti-progressive spirit versus dreaming of being in a green or new environment, which is indicative of progress or prosperity.

12. *How to Enhance Memory*: When you are awakened, if you cannot immediately remember your dream, do not become overly anxious. Instead, just lay still, meditate, pray, worship, or ask the Holy Spirit to bring back the dream to you. Dream recall may occur right away, or the Holy Spirit may bring it back to us later. Also, spiritual warfare giants will tell you to pray before going to bed and ask the Holy Spirit to cover your dream line. Notably, there are special areas of our brain that deal with memory,

Chapter 2: Tips for Dream Interpretation

so applying the blood of Jesus to these areas is certainly smart in protecting our memory from demonic intrusions.

All in all, even though our dreams may carry multiple meanings and must be interpreted within each specific context, using these twelve (12) interpreting tips as our guide when interpreting our dreams will give us a jump start to help us to unlock the mystery of our dreams. Now more than ever, we need to be dream sensitive and rule the sphere in our dream world.

CHAPTER 3:
NUMBER SYMBOLISM

"Knowing the meanings of numbers will allow us to be more aware of when favor and grace are being released for us as opposed to when evil blows are being sent to destroy our lives."

Many people can relate to having dreams concerning numbers, especially those who hold the office of a prophet or those who operate in the gift of prophecy. Therefore, having even a basic understanding of their meanings will be very impactful in helping us to unlock our dreams. In addition, please bear in mind that numbers may have different meanings based on cultures and traditions. For this reason, in this chapter, I will give you different viewpoints on the subject in focus.

El Elyon—*The Most High God*—is the greatest communicator, and He loves to communicate with people through the use of numbers. In Genesis 41, Pharaoh received a dream with the specific number seven (7). He dreamt of being near the Nile River and saw seven (7) attractive fat cows coming out of the river, which would be later eaten up by seven (7) ugly thin cows who came up shortly after. Similarly, the king had a second dream regarding the number seven (7) again; however, this time, it concerned seven (7) plump, good heads of corn being later devoured by seven (7) thin heads of corn.

This may sound ridiculous to you, but for Pharaoh, God was giving him a divine revelation of what was about to come. Pharaoh discerned that it was not "just a dream," and thus, his spirit was troubled. I can just imagine his psychological and emotional state being even greater troubled when none of the wise men or magicians were able to interpret his dreams (Genesis 41:8).

Thanks be to God! All was not lost because there was a young Hebrew man by the name of Joseph who had the anointing and gift of interpreting dreams. Even though he was in prison, "his gift would make room for him" (Proverbs 18:16). Joseph had the solution that was needed to put Pharaoh's anguish to rest, so he was quickly requested, and he rose to the occasion.

Joseph told Pharaoh that his dream represented seven

Chapter 3: Number Symbolism

(7) years of booming economy that would be shortly followed by seven (7) years of severe famine. Notably, interpreting Pharaoh's dream made Joseph receive a mind-blowing promotion—from the prison to the palace. Yes, a lucrative promotion that made him the head over Pharaoh's house and second (2nd) in command to Pharaoh on his throne. Furthermore, all Egyptians were ordered by the king to obey him. Still, Joseph also received a royal wife and abundant riches. He was given a once-in-a-lifetime opportunity to exercise his creative God-given leadership skills, and Joseph seized this opportunity. He used his ingenuity to design a first-world accounting system capable enough for storing and maintaining an excellent food supply for one of the most dangerous famines in Egypt's history. Of all the wise men in Pharaoh's time, only Joseph, the dreamer, or should I say, Joseph, the dream interpreter, was able to interpret and create a world-class system that would go down in the annals of history.

Interestingly, God is not the only one who uses numbers to deal with people, but the devil and his minions also employ their use. Thus, don't be deceived by the enemy and his allies, who happen to be the greatest deceivers and counterfeits. For example, many practitioners of the Dark Arts, such as witches, wizards, warlocks, diabolical priests and high priestesses, often cast spells by using certain numbers in their wicked practices. They are very skillful in incorporating numbers into their rituals to summon evil spirits to afflict people, especially in their sleep (dreams). Why do you think the Ouija board (an instrument used to communicate with the dead) has numbers on it? Dark Arts practitioners often use numbers with items (talismans), colors, and even drawing energies from the galaxies (or moon) to destroy people's lives. Why do you think the Bible says, "The sun shall not smite you by day nor the moon by night" (Psalm 121:6)? The enemy and his kingdom of darkness have incorporated the use of numbers to kill, steal, and destroy people's purposes and destinies.

Considering this, living a holy life and utilizing the gift of discernment becomes necessary to conquer the devices of the enemy. You must take your dreams and that of your loved ones more seriously. You must seek divine interpretation. The Bible says, "The people who know their God shall be strong and carry out great exploits" (Daniel 11:32, NKJV). The opposite is true; the people who don't know their God will be weak and will be exploited.

Having said this, from here onwards, whenever you receive dreams with numbers, you must pay attention to them like Pharaoh did and unlock their mysteries like Joseph. Knowing what each number means will put us in a better position to unlock our dreams. Still, knowing the meanings of numbers will allow us to be more aware of when favor and grace are being released for us as opposed to when evil blows are being sent to destroy our lives. Consequently, whenever you unlock your dreams with numbers that are favorable, it requires you to give God

Chapter 3: Number Symbolism

thanks and command them to speedily manifest through prayers and declarations. On the other hand, when you unlock dreams with numbers that are meant for your demise, you must rise like a military soldier and legislate a stop order to them. You must cancel and sever the evil intents of the enemy. Don't hesitate; in cases like these, delay means danger. Take authority with urgency and holy anger! Destroy the works of the darkness!

Let us now examine some numbers to specifically understand what each number symbolizes.

Number 0	Meanings	Additional Info
Christian	Zero (0) normally symbolizes *nothing, none, empty, and void.*	*Good sense:* "0" elevates any number when placed behind it; for example, 8 with zero behind it becomes 80. *Bad sense:* Dreams with "0" may be interpreted as uselessness, wasted efforts, lack of harvest, or lack of reward.
Jewish/ Hebrew	Zero (0) usually represents *what is hidden, uncertain, eternal, limitless, has great potential, is unquantifiable, and uncontainable.*	

Dark Arts practitioners	Those who practice the Dark Arts use Tarot cards to gain insights into one's past, present, and future. In Tarot cards, the very first card is assigned the number "0." This card is named "The Fool" and represents the individual about to begin a new journey, stepping into the unknown, which offers potential/choice. Ancient civilization embraced zero as the completion of a cycle. It is used to identify the point at which the potential of energy begins. Many see "0" as the womb, egg, or seed, which represents all life beginning. Zero (0) also symbolizes everything, absolute all, and eternity. In Numerology, "0" symbolizes the number of the "God" force/source. Zero also represents freedom from limitation in the material world.	

Number 1	**Meanings**	**Additional Info.**
Christian	One (1) generally represents primacy or state of being first, beginning, preeminent, and unity.	In monotheistic religion, one represents God or the oneness of the Godhead (Deuteronomy 6:4).

Chapter 3: Number Symbolism

Jewish/ Hebrew	The Hebrew words *achat and echad* are used for numeral one and symbolize *first, beginning, primacy, single, and oneness.* The corresponding pictographic meaning for one symbolizes *leader, first, strength, ox, chief, prince.*	
Dark Arts practitioners	In witchcraft, one (1) represents the intention of oneself. In magic, one (1) is used to focus on one person or to cast spells on one person or one family. In the Tarot deck, one (1) is The Magician's number and represents potential.	
Number 2	**Meanings**	**Additional Info.**
Christian	Two often symbolizes *commonality, purpose, or common interest.* It normally represents *joining in agreement, a union, covenant, marriage, reproduction, partnership, division, or the verification of the facts by witnesses.*	Genesis 7:9; Exodus 34:1, 4; Joshua 2:1; Matthew 18:19, 20; Galatians 4:24

Jewish/ Hebrew	The Hebrew words *shettayim and shenayim* are used for two and mean *difference, divide, oppose, judge, discern, witness, conflict, blessings, abundance, building, couple, and dying to self.* *Good sense*: two (2) normally represents *multiplication and blessings.* *Bad sense*: two (2) represents *division.* The corresponding pictographic meaning for two is *to build* a *house, tents, and son/daughters.*	
Dark Arts practitioner	Witches often invoke 2 when they need to bond two things together (mental or physical). In magic, 2 symbolizes a partnership or conflict with two opposing forces. Also, many work with the cycles of the moon to cast a spell; for example, they'll perform certain incantations or rituals when the moon is in its second cycle, thus burning two candles with evil intentions, repeating their actions/speech while holding two items which represent the persons they are casting a spell on (talisman).	Number two symbolizes dualities, e.g., me/you; good/bad; alive/dead; male/female; light/darkness; Yin/Yang. In the occult, 2 is the symbol of men, sex, and evil.

Chapter 3: Number Symbolism

Number 3	Meanings	Additional Info.
Christian	Three represents the number of the Godhead (Father, Son, and Holy Ghost). Three (3) also represents the triune man (Spirit, soul, body). Three symbolizes *intensify, treble, restoration in portions, threefold, three parts, three days, three years old.*	Jesus prayed three times in the Garden of Gethsemane before His arrest. (See Ezekiel 42:6; Ecclesiastes 4:12; Matthew 26:36–46; Revelation 8:13.)
Jewish/ Hebrew	The Hebrew words *shalosh and sheloshah* translate as number three and symbolize *trees, seeds, fruits, pattern, equilibrium, counsel, witness, revelations, strength, new life, sprouting, resurrection, fruitfulness, unity, chain of continuity, triangle, and foundation of the temple/house.* The corresponding pictographic meaning for three is *ripen, reward, nourish, mature, recompense, benefit, foot, and camel.* *Bad sense*: three (3) represents sowing seeds of discord and death, hands that shed innocent blood, and deeds/actions that tear down rather than gather and build (negative words).	

Dark Arts practitioners	Persons who practice Dark Arts see three (3) as a magical, mystical, and spiritual number. In the occult, spells are often recited three times as three symbolizes the cycle of a spell. Therefore, three black animals may be sacrificed in order to conjure up demons.	
Number 4	**Meanings**	**Additional Info.**
Christian	Four generally symbolizes *earth, world, and creation.*	Genesis 1:14–19; Ezekiel 1, 10; Revelation 19:4; John 11:39
Jewish/ Hebrew	The Hebrew words *arba* and *arbah* are used for the number 4, and like the number 7, they *symbolize completeness.* Four (4) also represents *authority, government, rule, calendar, creation, kingdom, dominion, time, fullness, giving of the law, and the Holy Spirit.* The corresponding pictographic meaning for four is *pathway, portal to heaven, door, knock, draw out or in, bow, branch, dominion, and control.* *Bad sense*: four symbolizes *a heart that devises wickedness, giving authority to the beast and evil desires.*	

Chapter 3: Number Symbolism

Dark Arts practitioners	Many witches create rituals for the four seasons and use portions like *Four Thieves vinegar* with the belief that by sprinkling it at strategic places, they will be protected. Dark Arts practitioners use the number 4 for "energies" to connect to the ruler of Saturn. In Tarot, the fourth card is The Emperor and represents control over your life.	Four also represents the order of the universe: 4 elements of the earth (earth, air, fire, water); 4 seasons (summer, winter, spring, and fall); 4 phases of the moon (full, new, half-moon waxing, and half-moon waning); also, the four cardinal points (east, west, north, south).
Number 5	**Meanings**	**Additional Info.**
Christian	Five represents *grace, goodness, favor, atonement, life, the cross, and fivefold ministries*.	Exodus 26 & 27; Matthew 14:17
Jewish/ Hebrew	The Hebrew words *chamesh* and *chamishshah* are used for numeral five and symbolize *power, strength, alertness, grace, Torah, service, gospel fruitfulness, anointed, going forth, fast move, movement, prayers, and protection*. The corresponding pictographic meaning for five is *breath, air, spirit, femininity, and behold to make known*. *Bad sense:* five represents *feet that run swiftly to evil, being ruled by the flesh*.	The Pentateuch (*penta* means five) refers to the five books of God's law (Genesis, Exodus, Leviticus, Numbers, and Deuteronomy).

Dark Arts practitioners	The number 5 was connected to the Babylonian goddess Ishtar (the goddess of war and sexual love). In occultism, the geometrical shape of a human placed in a circle with outstretched arms and legs is essentially the symbol of the five-pointed star or pentagram. This is used in summoning spells to trap a demon or devil to carry out the instruction of the sorcerer. Similarly, some witches also see the fifth element as the soul, and it represents the witch performing the spell.	Many witches use numbers to gain power or strength by secretly writing them down on their bodies or in hidden places or designs and making wishes when needed. Many people who practice darkness have five main appendages that, when spread, resemble a star. In the Tarot deck, the fifth card is The Hierophant, and it relates to school, marriage, alliance, captivity, and servitude.
Number 6	**Meanings**	**Additional Info.**
Christian	Number 6 represents *man, human weakness, Satan's evil, and the manifestation of sin.* The use of three *6s (666)* represents the number and mark of the beast, anti-Christ, Satan.	Genesis 7:6, Luke 13:14, John 2:6; 2:20, Revelation 13 and 18; Genesis 1, Exodus 20:9–11, Exodus 21:2–4; Deuteronomy 15:12; Leviticus 25:4; Exodus 23:10

Chapter 3: Number Symbolism

Jewish/ Hebrew	The Hebrew words *shesh and shishshah* translate to six (6) and symbolize *flesh, image, work, man, beast, connection, sacrifice, intimacy, knowledge, sacrificial love, antichrist, idol, Adam, relationship, and judgment.* The corresponding pictographic meaning for six is *nail, tent peg, hook, to connect, add to, and attach.* *Bad sense*: six symbolizes a *false witness that speaks lies.*	A Hebrew slave was to serve six years and be released in the seventh year. The land was appointed to be sown and harvested for six years.
Number 7	**Meanings**	**Additional Info.**
Christian	Number seven (7) represents *completeness and perfection, the foundation of God's word.*	Exodus 29:37, 43, 26; Leviticus 9:7; 16:14; Proverbs 9:1; Matthew 15:32–39; Mark 16:9; Revelation 1:4–18
Jewish/ Hebrew	The Hebrew words *sheba and shibah* translate to seven and symbolize *completeness, wholeness, ripe, order, stability, holiness, and rest.* The corresponding pictographic meaning for seven is *completion, plowshare, weapon, sword, adorn, feed, to cut, and to harm.* *Bad sense:* seven indicates tearing down the house by sowing discord.	

Dark Arts practitioners	In Numerology, the number 7 embodies vibration and energies, spiritual awakening and awareness, inner wisdom, inner abilities, and psycho awareness. Many people who practice evil work with astrological sciences to release curses on people. With this in mind, seven relates to lunar energy and connection to the moon.	

Chapter 3: Number Symbolism

Number 8	Meanings	Additional Info.
Christian	Eight represents *quantity or surplus, a new beginning, new order, or creation.*	2 Kings 22:1–2; John 20:26–29; Luke 9:28; Romans 2:28–29; Colossians 2:11–13; Matthew 14:25; Mark 6:48
Jewish/ Hebrew	The Hebrew words *shem-oneh and shemonah* translate to the number 8, which symbolizes *a new beginning, to make fat or to have more than enough; full to overflowing; moves from natural to supernatural.* The corresponding pictographic meaning for eight is new beginning, separation, *wall, fence, protect, sin, outside.*	There are a total of 8 watches used by Israel as a method of time keeping. Four-day watches and four-night watches. 1st watch (sunset): 6 p.m. to 9 p.m. 2nd watch: 9 p.m. to midnight. 3rd watch: midnight to 3 a.m. 4th watch: 3 a.m.– 6 a.m. (sunrise). 5th watch: 6 a.m.– 9 a.m. 6th watch: 9 a.m.– 12 (noon). 7th watch: 12 (noon)– 3 p.m. 8th watch: 3 p.m.– 6 p.m.
Dark Arts practitioners	Some practitioners connect eight (8) to the planet Mercury and say it gives messages from the divine.	

Please see the continuation of numbers in the appendix (at the back of the book).

CHAPTER 4:
COLOR SYMBOLISM

"The rainbow represents a covenant that God made with His people that He will never again destroy the earth with a flood."

El Shaddai—*God Almighty*—is our Creator and expresses His creativity using colors to showcase His innovations. I grew up on the words of a song that says, "All things bright and beautiful, / all creatures great and small. / All things wise and wonderful, / the Lord God made them all" ("All Things Bright and Beautiful," public domain). Indeed, how beautiful it is to see a rainbow screaming across the sky after rain showers, or better yet, the smiling sun peeking out from behind the clouds. Indeed, color is one of the ways in which God reveals His glory and communicates with His people. Without any exception, colors also play a significant role in our dream world. Therefore, having even a basic understanding of their meanings will assist us greatly in unlocking the mystery of our dreams.

THE RAINBOW COLORS

The rainbow consists of a myriad of colors, inclusive of red, orange, yellow, blue, green, and violet. In the Bible, the rainbow represents a covenant that God made with His people that He will never again destroy the earth with a flood (Genesis 9:13–17). Dreaming of a rainbow may indicate that God is establishing a covenant with you or a binding agreement that carries divine blessings, favor, and responsibilities.

PRIMARY COLORS

Red

Two Hebrew words, *adam* and *adom*, are used for "red" and mean "to show blood in the face" and "rosy," respectively (Strong, 2001). In the good sense, red normally represents *salvation, the love of God, humanity, and atonement.* On the other hand, red may also be associated with *warfare, blood sacrifice, or the shedding of blood* (Zechariah 1:8; Leviticus 17:11; Exodus 12:1–

Chapter 4: Color Symbolism

13; John 3:16–17; Colossians 1:20).

Thus, to unlock dreams with the color red, the dreamer must examine them within their context as well as looking at the cultural practices of the times. For example, a dream of someone killing an animal and its blood running at an altar may be linked to some form of ritual or witchcraft practices as opposed to someone giving you a red rose, which is indicative of love.

Blue

The Hebrew word *tekeleth* is used for blue. It was the color frequently used in the making of the priests' garments. In the good sense, dreams with the color blue generally symbolize royalty, riches, the Holy Spirit, God's healing, grace, heaven, and authority. Nonetheless, in the bad sense, dreams involving blue tones may represent physical punishment, hurts, wounds, and bruising (Exodus 24:10, 28:5–6; Numbers 15:38; Esther 1:1–6; Proverbs 20:30).

Yellow

Two Hebrew words used for yellow are *tsahob* and *y'raqraq*, and they mean "golden in color" and "yellowish-ness-greenish," respectively (Strong, 2001). Dreams with the color yellow may be positively associated with victory, revelations or insights, brightness, newness, and warmth (Psalm 68:13). In contrast, dreams with the color yellow may also have negative associations, inclusive of sickness and uncleanness (Leviticus 13:30). For example, dreaming of a baby looking yellowish (jaundice) must be unlocked through the lens of sickness as opposed to a dream of the rising of the sun or spring, which may be interpreted as newness.

SECONDARY COLORS

Green

One Hebrew word that translates as green is *lach*, which means "new, fresh, unused, undried or moist" (Strong, 2001). In the positive sense, dreams with the color green generally signify flourishing, freshness, new beginnings, growth, life, restoration, wealth, and prosperity. However, dreams with the color green in the negative sense may indicate *immaturity, inexperience, unfitness, unripeness, disappointment, and delays* (Judges 16:7–8; Songs 2:13; Psalm 23:2; Genesis 1:30).

Orange

One Hebrew word used for the color orange is *katom*. Orange generally symbolizes *danger, fire, and being tried and proven.*

Purple

One Hebrew word used for the color purple is *argaman*. In the good sense, dreams of the color purple often indicate *wealth, prosperity, royalty, status, kingship, and priesthood*. Nevertheless, in the bad sense, dreams of purple may be associated with *vanity, extravagance, and*

Chapter 4: Color Symbolism

mourning (Exodus 27:16; Judges 8:26; Esther 8:15; Luke 16:19; John 19:1–5; Revelation 18:12–16).

OTHER COLORS

Amber

Amber normally symbolizes the glory of God, His judgment, and endurance (Ezekiel 1:4).

White

The Hebrew word *lavan* is used for white. White generally symbolizes purity, holiness, redemption, rebirth, and the righteousness of Jesus Christ (Mark 16:5).

Black

Black normally symbolizes sin, darkness, mourning, death, and catastrophe (Zephaniah 1:15).

Silver

Silver often symbolizes the Word of God, divinity, redemption, salvation, and refining (Psalm 66:10; Psalm 12:6; Numbers 7:12–19).

Gold

Gold normally represents *kingship, royalty, glory, transcendence, God and His sovereignty, the refinement of the spirit, wealth, and spiritual power* (Revelation 14:14, Daniel 3:1, Matthew 2:11, Malachi 3:3, Haggai 2:8; 1 Peter 1:7; Revelation 21:18).

Scarlet

Scarlet generally represents *sin, immorality, prostitution, and adultery*. On the other hand, it also symbolizes *royalty, wealth, and power* (Daniel 5:16; Isaiah 1:18; Revelation 17:1–6).

Bronze

Bronze normally symbolizes *strength and durability* (Exodus 30:18; 1 Kings 7:23–26; Revelation 1:15).

Gray

The Hebrew word *afor* is used for gray. Gray generally represents *honor, age, dignity, and wisdom* (Proverbs 16:31; Genesis 42:38; 1 Samuel 12:2; Psalm 20:29; Psalm 78:18).

Brown

The Hebrew word *chum* is used for brown. Brown typically represents *the earth.*

Chapter 4: Color Symbolism

Pink

The Hebrew word *varod* is used for the color pink. Pink normally symbolizes *femininity and female rebellion.*

All in all, dreams depicting a particular color not only reveal the ingenuity of God but also can allow us to understand whether we are being attacked by the enemy during spiritual warfare. For this reason, we must pay keen attention to the different colors seen in our dreams, for doing so will give us more hints on how to effectively interpret our dreams and be ahead of the enemy's devices.

CHAPTER 5:
IMAGERY & SYMBOLS

"A dream with different or strange images must not be considered foolishness, for what it needs is proper unlocking to discover its worth."

Imagery and symbols are reflected throughout the Bible. It is indeed another means whereby God communicates with His people. Just to name a few, read the Books of Zechariah, Ezekiel, and Revelation to gain an appreciation for the different imagery and messages they convey. In sum, the first chapter of the Book of Ezekiel unfolds with imagery in all its splendor as the prophet receives a vision by the river of Chebar. The vision is of "four wheels" on a chariot drawn by four living creatures with four faces reflecting that of a man, lion, ox, and eagle. Today,

Ezekiel's vision would outdo any superb 4D movie as the appearance of the creatures were like burning coals of fire; their wings sounded like the noise of great waters, and when they moved, they reflected lights of lamps shooting out fire and flashing lightings. Talk about colors; there were burnished brass, terrible crystals, amber, and colors of beryl, to name a few. The vision culminated with the mention of a throne as an appearance of sapphire stones and Ezekiel being overtaken by God's glory, which caused him to fall on his face. Wow! What a climax indeed. Interestingly, this vision symbolizes God's divine authority, omnipresence, omnipotence, and providence and reflects him being the mighty warrior.

Like Ezekiel, the Book of Revelation is also dramatic as it reveals the apostle John on the isle of Patmos being given divine revelations by Jesus Christ about the end-time events (Apocalypse). It highlights a book in God's hand having seven seals being opened by Jesus, or the Lion of Judah, which ushers horses (white, red, black, and pale horses) and riders. The white horse and its rider are symbolic of conquest and the signaling of the entry of the anti-Christ. The red horse and its rider indicate end-time civil wars, while the black horse and its rider symbolize famine. The pale horse and its rider symbolize death and hell, which encapsulate the last judgment and the world coming to an end.

With this in mind, God continues to reveal His message to His people today in both dreams and visions. Therefore, a dream with different or strange images must not be considered foolishness, for what it needs is proper unlocking to discover its worth. When we do this, we become like a happy miner who discovers rare diamonds found a hundred miles deep in the earth's crust or way below the ocean's floors. No wonder diamonds are rare. Yes, a girl's best friend requires the average removal of two hundred and fifty tons of the earth to locate a single carat of diamond. Though difficult it may be, it's well worth the effort when we discover it, and so too when we unlock our dreams.

OCCULT SYMBOLS

From time to time, people get dreams of different imagery, which, when properly interpreted, may help the dreamer understand what battles they are up against. I will now attempt to share a concise amount of imagery and symbols used within the occult and other religions, which must be strategically unlocked when seen in dreams. Bearing in mind that some persons may deem a particular symbol as good, when Dark Arts practitioners are using them, they become dangerous weapons against people's lives. For example, while Christians use the Bible to glorify God, a witchcraft worker may use the Bible to carry out harmful rituals to kill and destroy.

PENTACLE/PENTAGRAM (5-POINTED STAR)

The pentagram is a popular occult or satanic symbol. It differs from the hexagram in that it carries five points. In occult practices, Dark Arts practitioners perform rituals and use the pentagram to conjure evil spirits. Notably, the five points connect to the five elements, namely: earth, fire, water, air, and soul. In light of this, during spiritual warfare, dreams with pentagrams may be indicative of evil powers being conjured to work against the dreamer and, thus, must be urgently nullified by the blood of Jesus Christ of Nazareth.

HEXAGRAM

The hexagram is used in many different religions worldwide and carries with it great controversy. Some people believe that the six-pointed star is the Star of David, thus connecting it to King David's famous shield and hence embracing the view that God is the protector. In contrast, many Christians and other Jews who lived through the holocaust (lived before World War II) or had family members who did believe the real history behind the six-pointed star is connected to Solomon. Solomon had a ring in which he could evoke evil spirits to do things for him (Testament of Solomon). With this said, occult workers and practitioners of the Dark Arts

Chapter 5: Imagery & Symbols

frequently use the hexagram to conjure evil spirits, which carry out their evil commands. In addition, hexagrams are also often used as talismans (objects used to harm or heal people through evil magical powers) by Dark Arts practitioners. Consequently, dreams involving hexagrams in the bad sense, then, are generally indicative of the Dark Arts or occult workers trying to hypnotize, seduce, and harm individuals. Once again, these dreams need urgent unlocking, powerful revoking by the Word of God and the blood of Jesus Christ of Nazareth.

SKULL HEAD

Another popular image is the skull, which is also seen on everything these days, including tattoos, belts, bags, clothing, and furniture. Recently, I saw a very popular entertainer with a clothing line of children's wear with skulls all over the collection. Dreams with skulls normally symbolize death or connect with the grave and powers of the dark world. These dreams also require urgent attention from the dreamer to pray against and ask God to revoke every satanic order of death against your assignments, destinies, purposes, communities, and loved ones. Be resolute, courageous, and strong like Joshua, and ensure that all evil covenants are smashed into irreplaceable pieces.

YIN-YANG SYMBOL

This imagery or symbol is very popular in Chinese philosophy and indicates dualities (up/down, male/female, etc.) as well as the harmony of heaven and earth. Therefore, it teaches that opposite forces are interconnected, interrelated, interdependent, and complementary. Yin is seen as female, dark, and negative, while Yang is male and represents light and the positive. Notably, some years ago, a man of God was coming under severe pressure in spiritual warfare and dreamt of *the Yin-Yang* symbol. The Holy Spirit helped the man of God to unlock the dream and revealed that evil moon deities were in operation. In other words, practitioners of the Dark Arts were releasing curses at night by connecting with elements of the moon. Thus, whereas many Chinese people celebrate this symbol, when it is used by Dark Arts practitioners,

Chapter 5: Imagery & Symbols

it can be very deadly as it is frequently associated with high-order demonic operations. To destroy these occult practices, the believer must employ the Word of God to quickly sever the evil attacks and seek daily to live a consecrated lifestyle (Psalm 12:6).

THE EYE OF PROVIDENCE

The eye within a pyramid has transcended into many cultures and religions worldwide today. It is frequently known as *The Eye of Providence*, *All-Seeing Eye*, *Spiritual Third Eye*, *The Evil Eye*, and *The Single*. Today, it can be seen on various tattoos all over the body (face, neck, chest, back, hand, etc.) as well as on nail arts and is even associated with famous musicians. The All-Seeing Eye is connected to its ancient Egyptian root practices and was popular during the fourth to sixth centuries, when kings' bodies were buried in magnificent Egyptian pyramids. Within this tradition, the Egyptians held the belief that so doing would preserve and protect them. Therefore, the Egyptians walked around with little idols and used the *All-Seeing Eye* for protection, good luck, and health. The Evil Eye is also associated with Freemasonry and Illuminati (secret societies). Different cultures and religions subscribe different meanings to it; nevertheless, within the occult, this symbol is most potent and dangerous. It is frequently used to summon demons and other evil spirits to carry out atrocities in people's lives—these include curses, hexes, psychic control, and other forms of divinations. Whereas the Eye of Providence is seen on the back of the USA's one-dollar bill and symbolizes the USA being watched over by God, for Dark Arts practitioners, it certainly carries a different meaning. For the occult, that All-Seeing Eye is ascribed to Satan, and all homage is given to him, which allows its workers to maximize their greatest evil powers for harmful practices. Consequently, the believer who is engaged in spiritual warfare must carefully unlock their dreams involving the "All-Seeing Eye" within its proper context and destroy the works of the darkness when necessary.

GOAT HEAD

The *Goat Head* is frequently worn as pendants on chains and other jewelry as well as employed in music history and is popularly seen on the covers of metal albums. The Satanists use this symbol to mock Christ as the lamb who died for mankind. Dreams of the Goat Head symbol are generally linked to *the Baphomet, horned god, god of witches, Satanists/satanic churches, the Goat of Mendes, and the Scapegoat.* These all indicate that occult works are in high operation; hence, why, once again, the dreamer must stay under the blood of Jesus while waging war against the kingdom of darkness. Also important is being fully armored or dressed for the battle, as outlined by the apostle Paul in Ephesians 6:11–18.

UPSIDE-DOWN CROSS

This symbol is used by many occult practitioners to mock and reject the cross of Jesus Christ. This is frequently worn on jewelry by many Satanists, musicians, and naive individuals who are not aware of the deceit of the enemy. Dreams of the upside-down cross normally represent that the enemy is insulting or mocking the child of God's faith and blatantly defying the power of Jehovah God. The dreamer must take authority and command every other spirit to be subject to the Spirit of the Almighty God.

TWO-FINGER SALUTE

This symbol is generally used for easy recognition among those who are in the occult and Dark Arts practice as well as certain types of music. Dreams of seeing this image when unlocked normally represent seduction, an invitation into demonic covenants or initiations into the dark world.

BIBLICAL SYMBOLS
Angels

Angels usually represent *God's messengers or ambassadors* (Genesis 16:7; Luke 1:26–28). To unlock dreams with angels, the dreamer must note the angels' message, appearance (color, size, temperament) as well as what the angels are doing (e.g., guarding, worshipping, etc.). Additionally, the key to unlocking these types of dreams concerns emotions. If you felt as if you were threatened or in danger of being attacked by the angel, it could very well be the enemy trying to deceive you as that angel may be a fallen one (demonic angel).

Bed/Bedroom

Dreams of a bed and bedroom in the good sense generally represent rest, intimacy, godly covenant, marriage, peace, and privacy. However, in the bad sense, they may symbolize evil covenants, idolatry, and sexual sins, inclusive of lust, fornication, and adultery (2 Kings 4:32–35; James 4:4; Revelation 2:22).

The Bible

The Bible is the Word of God, and dreams with the image of the Bible must be interpreted within this context. It is a symbol of divine revelations, light, and instructions. It also denotes worship and is the believers' defensive and offensive weapon. To unlock dreams with the Bible, pay keen attention to the size of the Bible, which may indicate the nature of the task. Also important to examine is what is being done with the Bible. For instance, pay keen attention to the text being read as this could be a message given to you by the Holy Spirit to build your faith, strength, hope, or to fulfill a specific assignment (Psalm 119:105–112; 2 Timothy 3:16–17).

Chapter 5: Imagery & Symbols

The Cross

The cross is universally accepted as the symbol of Christianity and is very dear to Christians worldwide as it symbolizes the finished work of Jesus Christ at Calvary. It, therefore, normally represents victory, triumph, salvation for humanity, dominion, and power. The cross is also seen as a symbol of sacrifice and everlasting love. Notwithstanding, or in the bad sense, it may represent pain and agony. The dreamer must pay keen attention to the type of cross and the activity being carried out; these will give the dreamer clues on how to unlock the dream (Matthew 16:24; John 3:14–15; Hebrews 12:2).

Crown

Crowns normally represent rulership, rewards, royalty or kingship, and eternal life. To unlock the dream, you must assess the type and size of the crown (e.g., diamond, gold, big, small, sparklingly) as well as what is being done with the crown (Proverbs 12:4; James 1:12).

Mantle

A mantle typically represents a covering, a robe, anointing, or license to act. It is symbolic in the prophetic and indicates power and authority to carry out assignments (Psalm 109:29; 1 Kings 19:19). To unlock dreams with mantles, examine what is being done with the mantle, its color, and size.

Rain

In the good sense, rain generally represents revival, life, blessings, the Holy Spirit, and the Word of God. Oppositely, in the bad sense, it may indicate trials and disappointments (Deuteronomy 32 2; Isaiah 55:10–11). Therefore, to unlock the dream, assess the type of rain, its impact on the dream as well as how you felt while it was raining.

Ring

Rings frequently represent authority, covenant, and eternity (Esther 1:6; Luke 15:22; Genesis 41:42). Here, size, type, color, and who is wearing the ring or being given the ring are keys to unlocking the dream.

Shoe/Slipper

A shoe/slipper usually represents *assignments, ease of motion, smooth, easy travel, or travel in general*. To unlock the dream, please pay attention to color, nature, design, and type (Joshua 5:15). The dreamer taking off the slipper in the good sense is indicative of a season of rest; however, in the bad sense, it normally represents setbacks, delays, or hindering of one's assignment.

Chapter 5: Imagery & Symbols

Water

Water generally represents *Spirit, refreshing, redemption, power of God, or the power of the enemy* (John 7:37–39; Revelation 12:3; Revelation 17:15).

To unlock dreams with water, the dreamer must take note of the condition of the water (stagnant or running, clean or dirty, spring, falls, pond, river, lake, or sea). Also important is the activity being performed in the water, as well as who or what is present in the water. Still, too, frequency, severity, and patterns must be examined. How frequently do you dream about water? How severe was the dream? How did you feel? Do you always dream of an old person beside the river? Answering these questions will help us to unlock the dream, to know if the dream is diabolical in nature or divinely inspired.

CHAPTER 6:
ANIMALS

"To effectively unlock dreams with animals, we must examine the creature's characteristics. Any dream involving being bitten must be canceled and severed immediately!"

Whether a roaring lion or a meowing cat, many people frequently encounter animals in their dream worlds. What does a barking dog represent as opposed to a growling wolf? Are animals really that important to take note of in our dreams? Well, we may not get that answer from the horse's mouth, but animals are very intelligent creatures and, for years, have been trained to carry out specific tasks with great success. This may sound unbelievable to you, but hear me out! Even recently, I read an article about how animals are now being trained to offer comfort to people in crisis. Talking about a catastrophe specifically, I read an article that outlined a heroic cat that led a rescue team to save an eighty-three-year-old woman who had fallen down a seventy feet steep ravine in Cornwall, England. If you have the opinion that a dog is a man's best friend, you better add to your catalog that a cat is now a woman's best compass. Presently, many homes would be so incomplete without these animals, which many have considered being members of their families.

The Bible, too, has given us some exciting stories about animals. Do you remember Jesus' triumphant entry on a donkey with the crowd shouting, "Hosanna!" in the highest (Matthew 21:1–11)? Likewise, what about Balaam in Numbers 22:21–39? The Bible reveals that Balaam's donkey saved him from being killed by the angel of God three times. Balaam, who was on a mission to curse the children of God, was interrupted by an angel. On the first occasion, the Bible says that when the donkey saw the angel with their drawn sword, it turned off the road. On the second occasion, the donkey squeezed Balaam's feet on a wall in order to avoid coming in contact with the angel. On the third occasion, when the donkey had no choice but to divert or move to one side of the road because the angel was immediately in front, the donkey stooped down, refusing to advance. Balaam, who was operating in the flesh, hit the animal on all occasions. The Lord allowed the donkey to speak to Balaam, asking

Chapter 6: Animals

him if it had ever been disloyal over the years. Balaam responded, "No," then the Lord opened his eyes, and he then saw the angel.

I could go on and on, from Samson to Daniel in the lion's den, but let's refocus on dreams. Are animals important for us to take note of in our dreams? Definitely! Can animals successfully carry out assignments? Well, if you are just finding out the answers to these questions, congratulations. There are persons who have been using animals for ages, not just to accomplish good deeds but also to wreak havoc in people's lives. Therefore, when you receive a dream with animals, it certainly makes sense to examine these dreams closely. Failure to do so may cost you dearly!

HOW TO INTERPRET DREAMS WITH ANIMALS

We have already established a few things in the previous paragraphs; notably, animals can be given and carry out assignments effectively. We have also established that animals are very intelligent; they can see, hear, and respond. In keeping with this, when we receive dreams concerning animals, in order to effectively interpret them, we must examine the creature's characteristics:

1. *Color*: What was the color of the animal?
2. *Numbers*: How many animals were in the dream?
3. *Temperament/Nature*: What was the nature of the animal? Was the animal loving or angry? What

was the animal doing? Was the animal staring at you? Was the animal advancing at you? Did the animal bite you? Was it attacking you?

4 *Location or Position*: What was the proximity of the animal? Was the animal on land or in water, above, beneath, beside, or around?

5 *Emotions*: How did the animal or dream make you feel during or immediately after waking from the dream?

Also, please bear in mind the other tips mentioned earlier and apply them when interpreting your dreams as well. Please note that even though the enemy is deceptive, the general principle still applies that once the animal is attacking or showing anger towards you, it indicates that the enemy is launching an attack. These dreams are not to be taken casually. Any dream involving being bitten must be canceled and severed immediately or within twenty-four hours. Failure to do so may severely affect your purpose and destiny and may even cost your life. Here's why: when a bite occurs, transference takes place; evil poison and toxins are released in the body that can paralyze or kill the dreamer.

Dark Arts practitioners often use animals to carry out evil intentions. Many dreams with particular animals represent high-order demonic attacks. I have listed a few of these below; please pay keen attention to them, especially if you encounter spiritual warfare. Pray aggressively. Break and destroy anything that is not of God. Use your available spiritual weapons to destroy and defeat the works of darkness in Jesus' mighty name. Let's now look specifically at some animals in greater detail.

BATS (CHIROPTERA)
Chief Characteristics

There are approximately 1,200 different species of bats. Bats are nocturnal mammals. They have the ability to hang upside down and to fly in this position excellently. In fact, they are the only mammals that can fly. These creatures use echolocation or soundwaves to see in the dark. They make noise and then fly based on the soundwaves that bounce off objects. Vampire bats bond by sharing regurgitating blood from animals mouth to mouth with other bats. More than one hundred different viruses have been associated with bats. Some of the severe ones include rabies, severe acute respiratory syndrome (SARS)—like coronavirus—and Ebola (Seltmann et al., 2017).

Unlocking the Dream: What Do Bats Represent?

Bats generally symbolize *witchcraft, darkness, death, and hatred.*

How to Pray

You must come against every hunter of the night. Announce that no vampire bat will draw your virtue by sucking your blood. Command these demonic bats to fall and die.

Command every witchcraft power to backfire now in

Jesus' mighty name. Ask the Holy Spirit to interrupt the soundwave of every diabolic bat and command confusion to overtake the enemy now. Use the fire of God to annihilate every eavesdropping spirit and announce you shall not be monitored in Jesus' name.

BEARS

Chief Characteristics

This powerfully built animal carries ten toes with curved claws and may stand erect on its hind feet to see and smell better. Even though its vision is poor, its sense of smell is sharp, and hence it frequently uses its nose to find food. Despite their huge size, bears can climb and swim well. Many male bears sometimes kill and eat their cubs. Nonetheless, female bears protect their cubs and normally attack humans, especially if their cubs are threatened. Notably, conflicts between bears and humans occur frequently in some natural parks in Japan. As a matter of fact, two hikers were injured in Ozegahara in 1999 and in 2004 (Hashimoto & Anrui, 2017).

Unlocking the Dream: What Do Bears Represent?

Bears generally symbolize *evil, an evil curse, opposition, danger, cunning, cruelness, or strongmen* (Hosea 13:8; Daniel 7:5; Revelation 13:2).

Chapter 6: Animals

How to Pray

Call on El-Shaddai *(Lord God Almighty)* to let every demonic bear be struck down immediately! Bind the strongman and declare whatever you bind on earth be bound in heaven, in the powerful name of Jesus (Matthew 18:18). Ask the Heavenly Father to send twelve legions of angels to oppose your opposers and to annihilate the evil one. Plea the blood of Jesus and shut down the nose of every demonic bear from locating you or your loved ones. Command every evil curse operating against you to break immediately in the powerful name of Jesus.

BLACK PANTHER (PANTHERA PARDUS PANTHERA ONCA)

Chief Characteristics:

Another fascinating animal is the black panther, which is known for its excellent swimming, running, hunting, and ambush skills. In fact, these large cats normally hunt at night, whether from the ground or trees. With their melanistic color or dark fur, they often camouflage in their surroundings and dismantle their prey in seconds. Depending on the region, whether Africa, Asia, or America, this silent predator is also called black leopard or black jaguar, respectively. In fact, the jaguar (black panther) is known as the largest South American cat (Viau et al., 2020).

Unlocking the Dream: What Do Panthers Represent?

Panthers usually indicate *high-order demonic forces that will try by stealth or undetected ways to come into your life*. This animal is not only dangerous in the physical but also in the spiritual and is commonly connected to witchcraft and occult practices.

How to Pray

You must pray and ask the Holy Spirit to expose and destroy every deceptive demonic spirit by fire. Ask the Lord to arrest and annihilate every demonic spirit of stealth that operates in the night season to attack. Tell the Lord to cover you with His blood and dismantle the senses of this evil spirit so that it will not locate you. Announce that you are getting stronger while the enemy is getting weaker and weaker in Jesus' powerful name.

CAT

Chief Characteristics

Cats tend to sleep during the day and go hunting at night. They are crafty hunters who sneak upon their prey, making sure they are weak before they kill it. There are many different species of cats, one of which is called the sand cat. This small-sized desert felid weighs around two to three kilograms and is found in sand and stone deserts ranging from the north of Africa to Asia and the Arabian

Peninsula. It is well adapted to living in areas where the temperature is extreme, ranging from zero degrees Celcius to fifty-eight degrees Celcius and the area is arid (without water) (Pas & Dubey, 2008).

Unlocking the Dream: What Do Cats Represent?

Cats often symbolize *high-order demonic forces associated with witchcraft, witches and Dark Arts practitioners, bewitching, charm, deception, craftiness, and unclean spirit.*

Interestingly, Ancient Egyptians believed cats had magical powers and brought good luck to their owner. Consequently, cats were worshipped, and the penalty for killing them was death. Ancient Egyptians also believed that gods and goddesses could transform into animals; thus, the goddess Bastet was said to transform into a cat.

How to Pray

Ask Jehovah-Shammah *(The Lord Is There)* to be your present help in times of trouble. Activate Exodus 22:18 and command every witch, wizard, warlock, diabolic high priest, or high priestess to repent or die! Use the blood of Jesus to break every curse, charm, hex, and vex. Superimpose the blessing of Jesus to locate you over and against every evil curse in Jesus' name. Announce that you will not be bewitched or seduced from the love of God or the things of God. Command every other spirit to be subjected to the Spirit of the Almighty God and announce that no evil spirit shall rule over your life and loved ones.

CATTLE

Chief Characteristics

Female cattle are called cows, while male cattle are called bulls. Cattle normally swallow and regurgitate (re-chewed or "chew their cud") their food. These animals can be shy, bold, or aggressive. Their vision and hearing are very good, and their taste buds allow them to differentiate between salty, sweet, sour, and bitter. Notably, there are more than 1.5 billion cattle worldwide, with over 105 million cattle raised in Canada and the United States alone (Brito et al., 2020).

Unlocking the Dream: What Do Cattle Represent?

In the good sense, cattle normally symbolize *wealth*. On the other hand, in the bad sense, cattle may represent *rebellion, aggression, poverty/scarcity/lack* (Exodus 32:4, 8; 1 Kings 12:28, Isaiah 7:21–25). Interestingly, in some cultures and religions, cattle are revered or worshipped. These animals are seen as a symbol of the pagan mother goddess and a symbol of psychic divination.

Chapter 6: Animals

How to Pray

Ask Jehovah-Jireh *(The Lord Will Provide)* to supply all your needs according to His riches in glory (Philippians 4:19). Command multiple streams of income to locate you and your bloodline. Announce that any psychic, witchcraft, or evil powers working against your wealth are frustrated in Jesus' name. Command every evil bull to fall down and die like Goliath. Announce that the spirit of rebellion shall not rule over your life nor the spirit of scarcity or lack. Activate Psalm 50:10 and ask the Almighty God to give you cattle on a thousand hills, a blessing of wealth.

DOG

Chief Characteristics

Domestic dogs have been associated with humans for at least 15,000 years, and some communities' identities have even been shaped by the reliance upon dogs for hunting. Dogs have superb hearing and an incredible sense of smell. They are often used to sniff out drugs, money, people, and even medical problems such as seizure attacks. Many are incredible swimmers and are also built to chase; therefore, some can run up to forty-five miles per hour (Rankine, 2018).

Dream Encounters with the Demonic Dog Spirit

A woman of God reported dreaming of a big strong black dog in her past community. She explained that the dog was seated on a verandah (front patio) but immediately attempted to jump on her shoulder upon her arrival on location. However, there was some unseen barrier that prevented the dog from biting her. For this reason, the dog only managed to mess up her clothes with its paws. The dream ended with the dog's owner quickly rushing to her. She assisted her in cleaning her clothes and gave her a reward.

Unlocking the Dream: What Do Dogs Represent?

Dogs symbolize evil or wicked people, fierce and cruel enemies (Psalm 22:16, 20).

In the natural, dogs are often labeled as "a man's best friend." Nevertheless, in spiritual warfare, they can be a man's worst enemy. Notably, Dark Arts practitioners frequently use dogs to attack or wreak havoc in people's lives. Therefore, dreams of dogs chasing, advancing, or biting must not be taken lightly. These dreams indicate a warning of impending danger of high-order demonic forces in operation, which must be destroyed before they destroy you. (Please see my spiritual warfare book entitled *Kill That Dog: Deliverance from the Dog Spirit* for a more comprehensive viewpoint on dog dream analysis.)

To unlock this demonic dog dream, we must pay keen attention to the setting or place where the dream occurred. Dreams involving former communities normally are associated with anti-progressive demonic spirits trying to restrict the individual. Also important is where on the

Chapter 6: Animals

physical body the animal attacked as well as the color, size, and strength of the animal. Notably, black symbolizes catastrophe, death, and darkness. Therefore, a black dog is indicative of danger and aims to kill or destroy.

In this dream, the dog only managed to jump on the woman of God's shoulder. Bearing in mind that the dog represents an evil person, strongman, or demonic spirit while the shoulder represents authority, we may interpret the dream as some powerful evil person/strongman/demonic spirit from her former community or past trying to kill or destroy her authority or sphere of influence (family, businesses, wealth, and destiny). However, the Spirit of God lifted up a standard as there was an unseen barrier that prevented the animal from carrying out its evil intentions. Thus, the unseen barrier represents the protective armor of God, shielding the woman of God from the enemy's mouth.

Even though the woman of God had suffered some setbacks by her clothes being messed up by the dog, her dream ended in triumph as the dog's owner quickly came and cleaned up her clothes and gave her a reward. Consequently, this suggests that the individual must never give up when faced with attacks or challenges in their sphere of influence. They must persevere despite the attacks of the enemy because, in the end, they will receive the reward. In other words, "No weapon formed against them shall prosper! The enemy may attack them, but he will not prevail against them, as God has not given them over unto death" (Isaiah 54:17; Psalm 118:18).

Dream of Dog Licking a Baby's Mouth

Dogs are sexual spirits used by cultic people to afflict people's lives. A dream of a dog licking a mouth represents the enemy trying to contaminate your gift/ministry, anointing, and purpose. In addition, the enemy may also be using some past sexual spirit to harass your life to prevent newness or breakthroughs from manifesting.

Functions of Demonic Dog Dreams

1. To deceive people
2. To make people worthless by drawing away or destroying their blessings.
3. To destroy people's health (physical, emotional, spiritual, etc.)
4. To destroy people's purpose (frequently works with a spirit of abortion)
5. To destroy people's peace (bombarded by fear and torment)

How to Pray

Pray against every ministry killer/destiny killer. Bind the strongman. Bind every evil contaminator. Repent for allowing the enemy access to contaminate your gift or calling. Renounce/revoke every attachment that was previously formed. Replace every evil attachment with the righteousness of God. Bind and destroy every sexually perverted spirit.

DONKEY

Chief Characteristics

Donkeys are mammals that are commonly used as work animals because they have the ability to carry heavy loads. Commonly known as "beast of burden" with a cross on their shoulder, they are usually gray, white, or black in color. Donkeys have been known to be used in carrying out railroad constructions, farming, mining, and natural resource extraction. Australia holds the world's largest population of free-roaming donkeys (approximately five million), Brazil is second with approximately 800,000, and the USA third with approximately 14,975 (Clancy et al., 2021).

Unlocking the Dream: What Do Donkeys Represent?

In the good sense, donkeys represent *humility, gentleness, patience, authority, wealth, industry, transportation, and dependability* (Genesis 12:16, 24:35; Genesis 30:43, Numbers 22, Isaiah 1:3, Job 1:3, 6:5, 42:12). Conversely, or in the bad sense, donkeys symbolize *stupidity, stubbornness, and poverty* (Exodus. 23:4; Job 39; Psalm 104:11).

How to Pray

Ask Adonai *(Our Lord and Master)* to keep His hands upon you so that your life will be forever governed by

His Spirit of humility and patience. Activate Galatians 5:22–23 anointing in your life and embrace the fruit of the Spirit: *love, joy, peace, longsuffering, kindness, goodness, faithfulness, gentleness, and self-control.* Fast and pray to break every spirit of stubbornness from your bloodline and declare that the spirit of stupidity is far from you. Ask the Holy Spirit to cover your industry, let you become a certified giver, a wealth distributor, and command every poverty spirit to be destroyed permanently by fire!

FOX

Chief Characteristics

Another dangerous animal is the fox; its physical appearance consists of thick or sparse furs, sharp canine teeth, long jaws, and muzzles. Foxes are skillful in digging holes and hence mostly live in underground holes. Foxes often kill and suck the blood of lambs. These omnivores are skillful hunters, scavengers, and thieves who eat just about anything. Their diets frequently consist of medium and small mammals, grass, small twigs, earthworms, insects, and birds (Baker et al., 2006).

Unlocking the Dream: What Do Foxes Represent?

Foxes represent cunning, sly, and evil men (Luke 13:32; Ezekiel 13:1–4, 2:15).

Chapter 6: Animals

How to Pray

In any dream with foxes, the dreamer must bind and cast out this demonic spirit that comes to creep up and destroy destinies. Ask the Holy Spirit to expose your enemies by fire. Let the God of heaven's angel army annihilate this cunning demon. Legislate that no weapon formed against you from the underworld shall prosper in Jesus' mighty name.

GOAT
Chief Characteristics

Goats are mammals with horns and short tails. Male goats usually have beards and are called "billy," while female goats are called "nanny." Goats' habitats include farmland, woodland, and mountains. As a matter of fact, mountain goats normally live in steep, mountainous environments where resources are seasonal (Kroesen et al., 2020).

Unlocking the Dream: What Do Goats Represent?

Dream of goat? Well, goats are generally connected to *lust, lewdness, sin, sinners, sin offering, and bestial sexual practices*. Goats also represent *cruelty, brutality, and perversions in the demonic world* (Leviticus 4:23; Ezra 8:35).

How to Pray

Ask Jehovah-Nissi *(The Lord Our Banner)* to put special protection around you to keep you from sinning. Use the blood of Jesus to cover your mind, body, soul, and spirit from all lust, lewdness, and sinful practices. Confess your sins and command every spirit of perversion to be forever broken from your bloodline. Ask the Holy Spirit to expose every evil strongman and to send the angel of God to ward off every spirit of brutality. Use the Word of God to cripple and paralyze every stubborn, tormenting evil spirit.

HARES

Chief Characteristics

Hares are swift animals that can run up to fifty miles per hour over short distances or up to thirty-five miles per hour over longer distances. Some hares can leap up to three meters (ten feet) at a time. These animals usually do not live in groups but live in simple nests above the ground. In Scotland, mountain hares are traditionally hunted for sport and killed to protect habitats such as young forests as well as to control the spread of the Louping-ill virus transmitted to red grouse (Hesford et al., 2020).

Unlocking the Dream: What Do Hares Represent?

Notably, the hare normally represents *uncleanness, Satan, and his evil spirits* (Leviticus 11:6; Deuteronomy

14:7). Many cultures embrace the notion that hares can be seen in the pattern of dark patches on the moon (moon rabbit). Consequently, practitioners of the Dark Arts may conjure whatever demonic forces to intrude and afflict people's lives. With this said, the dreamer must be vigilant and nullify any demonic hare attacks.

How to Pray

Activate Psalm 121:6 (NKJV) and declare, "The sun shall not strike you by day, nor the moon by night." Command every unclean spirit to fall and die in the powerful name of Jesus. Release the fire of God against the enemy's camp and command the sword of God to sever the feet of every swift animal. Ask the Holy Spirit to attack your attackers and pursue your pursuers in Jesus' mighty name.

HORSE

Chief Characteristics

Horses have large eyes located at the sides of their heads, which match their speed and body size. They have exceptional memory, vision, and hearing. As a matter of fact, their hearing is superior to that of humans, and they can hear without turning their heads. Still, horses have the ability to travel on their tiptoes, and some are even able to run up to approximately fifty miles per hour. Furthermore, wild (feral) horses in Australia have escaped domestication (taming) and since then have become an over-abundant pest in many environments destroying flora and fauna as well as negatively impacting water quality and soil compaction and erosion (Hobbs & Hinds, 2018).

Unlocking the Dream: What Do Horses Represent?

In the good sense, horses generally symbolize *swiftness, strength, power, spiritual support, and victory.* In contrast, in the bad sense, horses normally indicate *war or spiritual warfare, catastrophe, and death* (Revelation 9, 19:19; Job 39:19; Jeremiah 8:6; Psalm 32:9; Zechariah10:3).

Dream Encounter with Horse

Phillip (pseudonym) reported having a dream with a black horse that went into a pool and then later came out transformed into a golden horse. The golden horse was now wearing metal armor. The man of God said he felt protected in the dream.

To unlock this dream, you must pay attention to the color transition of the horse from black to gold. Black usually represents *sin, darkness, and death*, while gold represents *spiritual power, the refining of the spirit, and transcendence*. The changing of the color of the horse as well as going into and coming out of the water signifies that some transformation occurred or will occur in the person's life. It's like a baptismal experience, a refining of the spirit. In addition, the golden horse coming out with metal armor also symbolizes *strength, power, and protection*. All in all, some spiritual transformation has taken place or will occur in the man of God's life that will give him power, protection, strength, and support: such an amazing experience.

How to Pray

Ask Jehovah-Raah *(The Lord Our Shepherd)* to protect like the psalmist David and secure you from every catastrophe, war, danger, and death. *Tell Him to send you help from His sanctuary and strengthen you from Zion (Psalm 20:2).* Make intercession, ask sweet Jesus to cover you with His precious blood and allow you to conquer the enemy in every warfare. Ask the Holy Spirit to make your feet steady and sure to be the victor and not the victim in every battle (Habakkuk 3:19).

LEOPARDS (PANTHERA PARDUS)

Chief Characteristics

These strong beasts are skillful climbers and excellent communicators. Many times, they carry their meals with them up in the trees and, while communicating, make distinctive sounds inclusive of growls, purrs, or raspy coughs. Leopards are also clever hunters and often stalk down their prey very quietly and then pounce on prey, taking it down by biting its neck or using its felon paws. They also have excellent speed, running up to fifty-eight kilometers per hour and leaping six meters forward in the air, the size of three adults lying head to toe. These beasts spend most of their time alone, hunt at night, and camouflage in trees or caves during the day. Of all the large cats, leopards are the most widely distributed, ranging from Africa to the Russian Far East (Mondol et al., 2009).

Unlocking the Dream: What Do Leopards Represent?

Leopards normally symbolize *swiftness, cruelty, vengeance, ferocity, ruthlessness, and power* (Jeremiah 5:6; Daniel 7:6; Habakkuk 1:8; Revelation 13:2).

How to Pray

Announce that no other power is stronger or mightier than El-Gibhor *(Mighty God)*. Ask the God of heaven's angel army to ruthlessly wipe out every demonic leopard. Activate Psalm 35 and ask the Lord to take vengeance on high-order demonic spirits. Command every evil communication system to be disrupted and disconnected in the mighty name of Jesus. Ask the Holy Spirit to expose every evil leopard spirit and strike them with the lightning of God. Ask sweet Jesus to camouflage you in His blood.

LION

Chief Characteristics

Lions are qualified as "kings of the jungle" because of their pride, strength, and fierceness. They are great hunters whose signature is to roar and confuse their prey. As a matter of fact, a lion's roar can be heard from approximately five miles. Lions' eyes are able to adapt to the dark and consequently do most of their hunting at night and even find pleasure hunting in the midst of a storm. Notwithstanding, lions are more likely than spotted hyenas or leopards to kill livestock during the day. They hunt for their food and can eat up to forty kilograms of meat in a day. Their tongues also have sharply pointed rasps, which allow them to scrape meat off bones. Lions also kill humans (Creel et al., 2013).

Unlocking the Dream: What Do Lions Represent?

The lion represents *kingship, royalty, rulership, strength, courage, boldness, and good or evil persons* (Proverbs 30:30; Proverbs 28:1; 1 Peter 5:8; Revelation 5:5; Daniel 7:4; Daniel 6:16–24).

How would you interpret a dream of being thrown into a lion's den? Once again, you must pay attention to the context of the dream. A dream of being thrown into a lion's den definitely is a serious one and indicates danger. This dream could mean that an evil strongman wants to destroy your life as lions come to slay. As a matter of fact, they are known as the kings of the jungle because of their strength and fierceness. To overcome this attacking demonic force in your dream world, you must be bold like Daniel and exercise your spiritual authority like Jesus.

How to Pray

Ask Jehovah-Sabaoth *(The Lord of Hosts)* to tame and extinguish every evil lion. Use the sledgehammer of God to destroy the teeth of every evil lion. Use the sword of God to sever the tongue of every diabolic lion. Ask the Holy Spirit to blind the eyes of every satanic lion. Ask the Lion of the tribe of Judah to roar and confuse the sound of every confusing spirit in Jesus' miraculous name.

MONKEY (MACACA FASCICULARIS)
Chief Characteristics

Monkeys are omnivores whose bodies are covered with hair and can be dangerous, as they give terrible bites and transfer dangerous diseases. Generally, monkeys live in the forest, and they rely on their arms to swing from branch to branch. Interestingly, some monkeys can swing up to thirty-four miles per hour. As a matter of fact, the sakis or saki monkey that is commonly found in the tropical forest of South America, Ecuador, Peru, Bolivia, and Brazil is labeled as the "flying monkey" because of their speed and secrecy as they have eluded researchers for decades (Marsh, 2014).

Unlocking the Dream: What Do Monkeys Represent?

Monkeys represent *stubborn evil strongmen, ancestral demons/battles, or the enemy*. If you dream of a monkey, you must assess how the monkey made you feel as well as what the monkey was doing. Many times, the enemy uses the spirit of a monkey to drive fear or trigger anxiety in people's dream world. If the monkey bites you, you must neutralize that bite with the blood of Jesus and destroy every demonic sickness.

How to Pray

Bind every demonic strongman. Command them to fall and die. Repent on behalf of the previous generation and ask the Holy Spirit to destroy every evil ancestral covenant that was established. Use your spiritual weapon and strike the head of every evil monkey and command them to be destroyed forever.

PIGS (SUS SCROFA)

Chief Characteristics

A female pig is called a sow, while a male pig is called a boar. Wide areas of Asia, Europe, and North Africa are inhabited by wild boars and include around twenty-seven subspecies (Hongo et al., 2002). Pigs are generally considered greedy based on how they consume food. They are also labeled dirty, stink, or filthy in many cultures because they are often found or live in muddy, feces-filled environments without being bothered.

Unlocking the Dream: What Do Pigs Represent?

Pigs generally symbolize *uncleanness, ignorance, hypocrisy, religious unbelievers, and unclean people* (Deuteronomy 14:8; Matthew 7:6; 2 Peter 2:22; Proverbs 11:22; Isaiah 66:3).

How to Pray

Ask Jehovah-M'kaddesh *(The Lord Who Sanctifies)* to cleanse and make you holy with the blood of Jesus. Command every demonic unclean spirit to loosen its hold on your life in the miraculous name of Jesus Christ of Nazareth. Ask the Holy Spirit to expose and destroy every hypocritical spirit that is operating against you in the mighty name of Jesus. Destroy every attack of ignorance and annihilate that spirit with the illuminating light of Jesus. Command every unclean touch or evil penetration to be neutralized and nullified by the blood of Jesus. Ask the Holy Spirit to connect you with the right people to keep your mind, body, soul, and spirit clean, focused, and strong in Jesus' powerful name.

RATS (RATTUS RATTUS/RATTUS NORVEGICUS)

Chief Characteristics

There are over sixty species of rats. Rats are omnivores that are covered in fur and eat just about anything in their environment. These rodents have an excellent sense of smell and can travel up to eight miles per hour. They are mammals that live in trees, near rivers, sewers, drainage, undergrounds, attics, and basements. Rats often carry and spread diseases to animals and people as they bite when they feel threatened. Furthermore, when humans come in contact with rat feces and dead bodies, these can also be infectious. Some of the diseases rats spread include rat-bite fever, hemorrhagic fever with renal syndrome, salmonellosis, and Lymphocytic Choriomeningitis (LMC) (Center for Disease Control and Prevention [CDC], 2017).

Dream of Rat Biting

One dreamer reported having a dream of being bitten in the back by a rat. Not surprisingly, later, the dreamer actually experienced real physical pain in the area where the rat had bitten in the dream. Another dreamer reported that her mom received a dream involving a rat biting her feet. What do dreams like these represent?

Unlocking the Dream: What Do Rats Represent?

In the dream world, rats normally evoke fear and anxiety. Rats usually represent enemies of progress. They normally symbolize familiar spirits and destroyers. Rats also represent witchcraft attacks, destructions, poverty, and lack. Dreams involving rats must be carefully examined because, as in the natural, demonic rats come to eat away just about anything in their environment. As a matter of fact, dreams involving biting must be pursued or countered with quick, aggressive warfare prayers. Similar to the natural, when rats bite in the spiritual, they are also transferring evil diseases. Hence, dreams involving biting signify that the enemy is launching attacks with sicknesses to cause the person's finance to leak out. To unlock the dream, please pay keen attention to where the rat bites or is nibbling. In this case, the rat bites the feet, which indicates the person's mobility is being threatened *(see further in the chapter about human anatomy on feet)*. Also, being bitten in the back may indicate backstabbers are at work.

Dream of Killing Rat

Some individuals may dream of killing a rat or crushing rats under their feet. What does this represent?

Unlocking the Dream

This is definitely a good dream as it indicates you have conquered your enemy. In other words, you have been victorious in destroying the destroyer or any spirit of lack that threatens your progress and dominion. What should you do? Rejoice and be exceedingly glad. Announce, "By this I know that You are well pleased with me, because my enemy does not triumph over me" (Psalm 41:11, NKJV).

How to Pray

Pray against every waster, devourer, backstabber, and

evil worker. Ask the Holy Spirit to expose and destroy every rat spirit by fire. Apply the blood of Jesus as well as your consecrated olive oil to the area where the rat has bitten, and ask sweet Jesus to flush out every contamination from your body with His blood. Bind and render powerless every demon of destruction, poverty, and lack by the power of the Holy Ghost.

TIGERS (PANTHERA TIGRIS)
Chief Characteristics

These carnivorous mammals are excellent hunters at night as they possess night vision that is six times better than humans. Still, their colors allow them to camouflage, as they easily blend in with the environment. They have powerful jaws and teeth that allow them to decisively attack and kill their prey. These big cats have mastered the art of slowly creeping and ambushing their prey by lunging at the animal's neck, sinking their teeth, and holding on until the prey dies from suffocation or bleeding out. Notably, if the tiger is unable to catch its normal prey as a result of illness or old age, it will turn to human consumption. Presently, the Indian subcontinent harbors around 60 percent of the current global free-roaming tiger population (Tyagi et al., 2019).

Unlocking the Dream: What Do Tigers Represent?

Tigers normally symbolize *occult power, high-order demonic forces* whose aim is to kill, steal and destroy (Job 11:4).

How to Pray

Ask El Eloah *(God Mighty and Strong)* to decisively attack your attackers. Command every hunter of the night to fall down and die. Use the fire of God to blind the eyes of every demonic tiger. Cry out for angelic assistance and ask the Holy Spirit to dispatch the angels assigned to warfare to locate, arrest, and destroy every camouflaging tiger. Announce that your virtue will not leak out. Use the thunderbolt of God to decisively destroy every suffocating spirit in the powerful name of Jesus Christ of Nazareth.

WOLF

Chief Characteristics

Wolves have keen senses, large canine teeth, powerful jaws, and the ability to run at thirty-seven miles per hour. Wolves are predators, and they are associated with *danger, destruction, and deception.* Many are aware of the fictional story of "The Big Bad Wolf," which is always up to some trouble, threatening to huff, puff, and blow the house down. Likewise, in reality, sharing space with carnivores no doubt will result in conflict with human activities such as livestock devastation (Landry et al., 2020).

Unlocking the Dream: What Do Wolves Represent?

Wolves typically symbolize *Satan, wicked and false teachers, wolfish, one who destroys God's flock* (Ezekiel

22:27; Jeremiah 5:6; John 10:12; Matthew 10:16; Acts 20:29; Luke 10:3; Matthew 7:15; Zephaniah 3:3).

Dreams with wolves must not be taken lightly as this demonic spirit comes to shed blood, destroy souls, and get dishonest gain (Ezekiel 22:27).

How to Pray

Ask El-Roi *(The God Who Sees)* to reveal to you every deceptive, destructive spirit in the blessed name of Jesus. Activate Psalm 23 and announce that *though you walk through the valley of the shadow of death*, you will fear no demonic wolf. Command the angels of God to cage every big bad wolf. Announce that your family, ministry, community, and business will not be destroyed by Satan or false teachers in Jesus' awesome name. Superimpose life over everything that belongs to you, and command every demonic wolf to die, die, die!

ARACHNID ANIMALS

SCORPION

Chief Characteristics

Scorpions have inhabited the earth for over 400 years and are classified as the first animal to transition from sea to land. They are mainly nocturnal and are plenty in deserts. There are more than over 1,700 species of scorpion, which are characterized by a segmented body with a curved tail. These arachnid species have a venomous stinger on the back of their body. As a matter of fact, their success is dependent on the production of potent and complex venom that they use mainly to kill and paralyze their prey (Ortiz & Possani, 2015).

Unlocking the Dream: What Do Scorpions Represent?

Dreams with scorpions normally symbolize *demonic operations*. Scorpions represent *pain, that which scourges; a whip, satanic* (Deuteronomy 8:15; 1 Kings 12:11; Revelation 9:5, 10; 2 Chronicles 10:11).

How to Pray

Ask the Almighty God to heal you of every wound, pain, or poisonous substance. Ask sweet Jesus to flush out your organs, tissues, cells, and blood vessels with His precious blood. Command every venomous serpent working against you to fall and die.

SPIDER

Chief Characteristics

Spiders are normally classified based on their eye arrangements and the types of webs they build. Most spiders have eight eyes, and their eye arrangements differ to reveal their type. Spiders are either hunters or gatherers. Their webs are made of silk, produced from spinnerets at the end of a spider's abdomen. These are used to spin webs, wrap prey, line their retreats, construct egg cocoons, and travel. The orb-weavers, cobweb spiders, and funnel weavers are the most popular web-building spiders. For the gatherer spiders, webs serve as the primary hunting tool. Most spiders are venomous and use their venom to immobilize their prey. Spiders' venom either impairs the prey's nervous system (neurotoxic) or dissolves their tissues (necrotic) (Durkin et al., 2021).

Unlocking the Dream: What Do Spiders Represent?

Spiders symbolize the *activities and shrewdness of the wicked* (Isaiah 59:1–8; Proverbs 30:28; Isaiah 59:5; Job 8:14). Dreams with spiders are either geared to entice, entrap, or ensnare the dreamer into bondage or a cage, as it is in the natural world, where the spider's victims are lured into its web and are entrapped, so it is in the dream world. Be vigilant and stop the spider spirit before it stops you!

How to Pray

Call on the God of Elijah to answer by fire, burn, and destroy every spiderweb now. Ask the God of Daniel to rescue you from every demonic entrapment. Use the blood of Jesus to loosen yourself from the snare of the spider. Ask the Holy Spirit to increase your discernment and to break you free from every evil enticement. Decree and declare that you will not be tricked by the enemy. Ask the God of Samson to give you supernatural strength to arise and destroy every deceiver in your life, in Jesus' mighty name. Command the volcanic fire of God to destroy every spider that comes to poison you in Jesus' name.

CHAPTER 7:
BIRDS

"Dark Arts practitioners often use birds as monitoring spirits as well as to carry out other evil intentions. Like dreams with animals, many dreams with particular birds often indicate when the enemy is launching an attack."

There is an old adage that says, "Birds of a feather flock together." Interestingly, birds are not just flocking together these days; they are also appearing in our dreams. What do birds represent? Can Dark Arts practitioners use birds to attack people in their dreams? Better yet, can God use birds to give us divine revelation in our dreams?

Well, birds have been mentioned many times in the Bible. In the Book of Genesis, after the first-ever great devastating flood, the Bible revealed that Noah sent out a raven that kept flying back and forth until the waters were dried up from the earth. He also sent out a dove to see if the waters had receded from the surface of the ground, but the dove could not find anywhere to perch because the water was all over the surface of the ground, so the bird returned to Noah. Noah waited seven more days and gave the bird the same assignment; this time, the dove returned with a freshly plucked olive leaf in its beak. This clever bird made Noah aware that the water had finally receded. Nonetheless, Noah, being wise, wanted to make certain, so he waited seven more days and then gave the bird the same mission. This time the dove did not return, allowing Noah to be fully convinced that it was now safe to descend from the ark (Genesis 8:6–12).

From a screaming vulture to a goblin' turkey or a trumpeting swan, like animals, birds are also intelligent and can be trained to carry out special assignments.

HOW TO INTERPRET DREAMS WITH BIRDS

In order to effectively interpret our dreams, when we receive dreams with birds, like animals, we must consider the creature's characteristics or features:

- *Color*: What was the color of the bird?
- *Numbers*: How many birds were in the dream?
- *Temperament/Nature*: What was the nature of the bird, loving or attacking? What was the bird

Chapter 7: Birds

doing? Was the bird chirping like a songbird or crowing like a rooster? Was the bird staring at you? Was the bird advancing at you? Did the bird pick you?

- *Location or Position*: What was the proximity of the bird? Was the bird in the air, on land or in water, above, beneath, beside, gathering around you? Another important thing to note is the position or location of the bird. Was the bird on a tree or on a pole?

- *Emotions*: How did the bird or dream make you feel during or immediately after?

By answering these questions and using the additional dream tips given earlier (determine the source, severity and intensity, frequency, time of occurrence, and patterns), you will become an expert in dissecting your dreams with birds. Notably, Dark Arts practitioners often use birds as monitoring spirits as well as to carry out other evil intentions. Like dreams with animals, many dreams with particular birds often indicate when the enemy is launching an attack. Nevertheless, I decree no weapon formed against you shall prosper. Let's now look at some of these intriguing birds.

DOVE

Chief Characteristics

Doves belong to the pigeon family and are known for their soft cooing and gentle walking. These birds have small heads and bills compared to their body. Doves are often white, gray, brown, or peach.

Unlocking the Dream: What Do Doves Represent?

Doves normally symbolize *gentleness, purity, and the Holy Spirit* (Matthew 3:6; John 1:32). Dreams with doves are normally good; nevertheless, please pay keen attention to what the birds are doing, as this will give you further insights on how to unlock the hidden mysteries. For example, was the dove aggressive in nature and advancing to pick you? Was the bird silent or cooing? Did you feel at peace because the dove was calm, or did you feel threatened because of the number of doves flying around you? Answering these questions will give you an understanding as to whether Dark Arts practitioners are using birds as familiar spirits to destroy you or whether the Holy Spirit is giving you insights and revelations.

How to Pray

Ask the Holy Spirit to manifest His glory in your life. Announce that you will continue to experience great fellowship with God. Proclaim that honor is your portion because you rule by humility and gentle spirit.

EAGLE

Chief Characteristics

Eagles are predatory birds that can live up to seventy years. They have keen vision and can see prey from long distances, even up to fifty miles away. Their eyesights

Chapter 7: Birds

are approximately five to six times sharper than humans. Eagles are also famous for soaring at high altitudes, even up to 10,000 feet.

These large striking birds are known as the kings of the bird family species. They do not devour dead things and normally flock with their kind. As a matter of fact, a golden eagle could expel three pairs of griffon vultures from a ledge to install their nest there (Reyes et al., 2020).

Unlocking the Dream: What Do Eagles Represent?

Eagles normally symbolize s*wiftness of flight, strength, power, majesty, and wisdom* (Job 9:26; Deuteronomy 28:49; Psalm 23:5, 30:19; Revelation 12:14; Psalm 103:5).

How to Pray

Ask the Holy Spirit to activate the wisdom of God in your life. Declare Isaiah 40:31 and announce that you don't mind waiting on the Lord and that as you wait, the Lord shall renew your strength. Proclaim that you shall run and not be weary; you shall walk and not faint. Ask the God of Abraham, David, and Joshua *to make your feet like deer to run through troops and leap over walls* (Psalm 18:29).

FOWL

Chief Characteristics

Fowl often live together in flocks and may gang up on weak or inexperienced predators. Fowls often come to lodge, pick, scatter, and fly.

Unlocking the Dream: What Do Fowls Represent?

Fowls typically represent *evil spirits/beings that come to lodge, pick, scatter, and destroy.* Fowls are frequently used by Dark Arts practitioners to perform rituals that involve blood sacrifice, and therefore dreams with fowls are often symbolic of witchcraft (Leviticus 20:25; Revelation 18:1–2; Mark 4:32).

How to Pray

Activate Psalm 35 and ask the Lord to fight against those who fight against you. Announce Exodus 22:18 and ask the God of heaven's angel army to inflict suffering and for not a witch to live. Bind and render every witchcraft attack powerless. Release the volcanic fire of God to burn and destroy every witchcraft camp. Ask the Holy Ghost to release missiles upon every demonic altar and permanently destroy the works of the devil.

Chapter 7: Birds

HAWK

Chief Characteristics

There are many different species of hawks, including red-tail, red-shouldered, sharp-shinned, and goshawk. Hawks are very intelligent, have excellent vision, and may perch on roadside poles or soar above looking for prey. Their diet consists of fish, lizards, snakes, mice, grasshoppers, crickets, rabbits, and birds. The northern goshawk is a forest-dwelling species that mainly preys on middle-sized birds in Europe (Burgas et al., 2021).

Unlocking the Dream: What Do Hawks Represent?

Hawks often represent *uncleanness* (Leviticus 11, 13, 16).

How to Pray

Ask the Heavenly Father God to close every door that the enemy wants to enter to contaminate your mind, body, soul, and spirit. Repent on behalf of yourself, your loved ones, and your bloodline. Ask sweet Jesus to cleanse and purify your life, ministries, bloodlines, and purpose with His blood. Announce that whatever belongs to you shall not be contaminated by the enemy. Destroy every demonic, ungodly covenant, and establish a new holy covenant with Jesus Christ of Nazareth.

OWL

Chief Characteristics

Owls are night birds that have the ability to fly almost soundlessly through trees because of their unique wings and feathered feature that reduces locomotion-induced sounds. These far-sighted birds also can see excellently in the dark. Owls have exceptional hearing as well, which allows them to hear prey from under leaves, dirt, and snow. These birds are masters of camouflage because their colors allow them to blend into their surroundings. Consequently, these predators often hide and then suddenly swoop down on their prey (Edut & Eilam, 2003). Their mouth is able to swallow prey whole. The owl killing is very gruesome; they often crush the prey, rip it up, or eat it whole. From hooting to squeaking, whistling, screeches, and hissing, owls are famous for making these terrifying sounds.

Unlocking the Dream: What Do Owls Represent?

Owls generally mean *wisdom, evil spirit, and demonic powers*. Dreams of owls normally come to trigger fear and anxiety in the individual's life. These dreams also signify that the enemy is launching an attack of death and destruction.

How to Pray

Ask the Holy Spirit to expose and destroy every camouflaged spirit. Bind every demonic sound and render

Chapter 7: Birds

every attack, confusion, and emotional disturbance powerless. Activate the sword of God and ask the Holy Spirit to chop off the wings and head of every demonic owl. Release the fire of God against every devouring spirit and announce that your joy, peace, health, wealth, etc., will not leak out. Make prophetic declarations that your blessings and breakthroughs will not be swallowed up by any demonic owl. Ask Jehovah God to deafen the ears and blind the eyes of every monitoring spirit. Declare that you shall not die, but you shall live with long life. Ask the Lord to release His angels to surround you.

PIGEON

Chief Characteristics

There are over 250 species of pigeons worldwide. They are distinguished from doves based on their size, with the pigeons often being the larger of the two. Pigeons are frequently characterized as (historical) messenger pigeons, homing pigeons, flying/sporting pigeons, racing pigeons, fancy pigeons, and utility pigeons. Still, did you know that pigeons are the source of several diseases that are transmissible to humans? Yes, when humans make contact with pigeon droppings, feathers, dust, and mites, they are at risk of receiving several pulmonary diseases such as allergic alveolitis, bronchiolitis, hypersensitivity pneumonitis, and others. Therefore, bird keepers are encouraged to wear gloves and masks when inside a pigeon's loft or house (Israili, 2017).

Unlocking the Dream: What Do Pigeons Represent?

The pigeon generally symbolizes *a mourner, sacrifice* (Isaiah 59:11; Leviticus 1:14; Genesis 15:9).

White pigeons, however, normally represent *peace and gentleness.*

How to Pray

Ask the Holy Spirit to crown you with peace and favor. Declare that no evil shall come near your dwelling. Proclaim that death and destruction must be far from you and the lives of your loved ones.

RAVEN

Chief Characteristics

Ravens are extremely smart birds that can imitate human speech even better than parrots. They sometimes lead wolves or foxes to carcasses in order to get the leftovers. These birds are easily adaptable to different environments inclusive of snow, desert, mountain, and forest. Given that they're known as scavengers, their meals include fish, meat, fruits, seeds, and garbage. They are known for distractions and tricking/stealing animals out of their food (Lanzendorfer, 2021).

Chapter 7: Birds

Unlocking the Dream: What Do Ravens Represent?

Ravens often symbolize *evil spirits connected with famine and confusion* (Isaiah 34:10–11; Proverbs 30:17; Matthew 13:3–23). Also, many cultures embrace a negative viewpoint of ravens from *messengers of the gods to murderers, souls of wicked priests, and Satan himself.*

How to Pray

Release the thunderbolt of God against every demonic raven. Ask the Almighty God to strike and destroy every spirit of distraction and legislate that you will not be tricked by the enemy. Ask sweet Jesus to cover everything that belongs to you under His precious blood from every demonic thief.

VULTURES

Chief Characteristics

Vultures are large predatory birds with wide wings, often bald heads, and bare necks. They are scavengers and mostly feed on dead or rotting carcasses. These birds are sometimes seen with other birds and animals when carcasses are too difficult to tear open by themselves. They often urinate on their legs to keep themselves cool when the time is hot. Vultures are excellent at soaring and looking for dead meat. These birds have an excellent sense of smell, which allows them to detect prey from miles away. Vultures have infinite patience; they will wait for days and weeks for an animal to die so they can devour it. They frequently perch in trees and on utility poles. During the days, they will fly very high so as to go undetected or undiscovered. When threatened, they vomit their food as a defense mechanism to lighten their body weight so they can fly and escape easily. These predators also prey on extremely sick, wounded, or infirmed prey. For example, vultures sometimes target disadvantaged animals or those giving birth to young (parturition), thus, tearing away genitalia and killing the calf or lamb (Reyes et al., 2020).

Dream Encounters with Vultures

Persons have reported dreaming of huge black vultures, perching way up high in a tree, motionless with serious penetrating eyes. Others have reported seeing a vulture hovering around the house of their childhood or former community.

Unlocking the Dream:
What Do Vultures represent?

Vultures often represent *unclean birds, evil spirits, or demonic powers*. Dreams of vultures can signify that the enemy is monitoring you to carry out an evil attack or monitoring to see if his evil plans that were set in motion are succeeding. Therefore, in spiritual warfare, dreams of vultures could indicate high-order demonic

Chapter 7: Birds

forces in operation. These dreams suggest that the enemy is geared toward bringing about death in every area of the individual's life, family, or loved ones, death of relationships, ministries, businesses, finance, passion, or purpose.

To unlock the dream, you must pay keen attention to the location and activity of the vulture. Was the vulture in the air hovering or waiting in trees motionless, staring to suddenly attack? Whenever I am attacked with depression, or loss of passion, energy, or creativity, a spiritual vulture bird is normally sent to fulfill such a mission in my dream world. Also important to note is the number of vultures seen in the dream. Still, if the setting of the dream depicts your former community, then the evil vulture bird was sent for you to remain backward or stagnant. Also, vultures perching on housetops represent death in that particular household.

How to Pray

Ask the Holy Spirit to open your spiritual eyes to detect every evil vulture from far-off. Bind every demonic vulture bird. If the vulture is perched in a tree, you must release your spiritual arsenal to destroy every attack from the tree and so forth. Dreams involving former communities require the individuals to aggressively pray and destroy every anti-progressive spirit that has been assigned to hinder their progress. Ask the Lord to anoint your hands for war and your fingers for battle to shoot down every vulture bird that is in high places hovering or perching. Activate Job 28:7 and ask the Holy Spirit to blind the eyes of every evil monitoring vulture. Use the fire of God to expose and burn these evil vultures and give them a new assignment to become the footstool of Jesus Christ. Use the sword of God to sever the head of these diabolic vultures and ask the Almighty God to cage them in the abyss. Ask the Holy Spirit to let every evil bird be tormented forever and cause their plans to fail miserably.

CHAPTER 8:
INSECTS & REPTILES

"The key to the unlocking of dreams with insects and reptiles centers on the characteristics of the creature, inclusive of the amount, size, type, and attitude."

Many people have encountered ants, roaches, alligators, lizards, and snakes in their dream worlds that, no doubt, evoke great fears and anxieties. The fact is that some insects and reptiles can be very dangerous in the natural/physical realm, which, likewise, can even be more dangerous in the spiritual realm. With this said, it then becomes vitally necessary for the dreamer to properly unlock their dreams involving insects and reptiles so as to gain greater insights and become the victor and not the victim. Importantly, the key to the unlocking of dreams with insects and reptiles centers on the characteristics of the creature, inclusive of the amount, size, type, and attitude (friendly, angry, attacking, blocking). Equally important are their locations and settings (air, land, sea, tree, building, dirty, clean, and so on). Having said this, the author desires that this chapter will give you great revelations concerning your dreams of insects and reptiles. It is about time for us to take authority even while sleeping or dreaming. Let us rise up and rule over every creature, whether crawling, flying, or swimming!

ANTS

Chief Characteristics

Ants have compound eyes, which are used for acute movement detection. Their heads carry many sensory organs that are used to get information from the external world.

Unlocking the Dream: What Do Ants Represent?

In the good sense, ants generally represent *industriousness and wisdom* (Proverbs 30:25, 6:6–8).

Conversely, or in the bad sense, spiritual warfare giants will tell you that ants are often connected to witchcraft practices. Therefore, dreams of black ants normally symbolize *death*, while red ants generally symbolize *great pain and afflictions*.

How to Pray

Bind every demon of death and render their assignments powerless. Superimpose life over and against death by activating Psalm 118:17 (KJV) and Psalm 91:16 (KJV) and declare, "I shall not die, but I shall live with long life." Enforce Isaiah 54:17 (NKJV), "No weapon formed against [me] shall prosper." Rebuke every graveyard spirit and send it back to the enemy's camp. Command every witchcraft spell to be permanently broken in the mighty name of Jesus.

COCKROACHES
Chief Characteristics

Cockroaches are disgusting insects that are usually found in dark, dirty places. These six-legged two antennae pests invade many people's spaces and are recyclers of decaying organic materials. Cockroaches are carriers of various diseases, and even debris off their skin can cause people to have allergies. They emit both unpleasant sounds and odors. Some have wings to fly, which aid their ability to enter homes by any means possible.

Unlocking the Dream:
What Do Cockroaches Represent?

Cockroaches usually represent *pollution, evil order, sickness, disgrace, and environmental witchcraft.*

How to Pray

Repent of any sin that gives the enemy legal right to afflict you. Ask sweet Jesus to cleanse your life of all evil pollutions with His blood. Command any evil cockroach assigned against you to be crippled and die in the mighty name of Jesus. Make a prophetic declaration that any witchcraft powers assigned against your progress be destroyed now, in the mighty name of Jesus. Ask our sovereign Lord to dismantle every evil coven and torment your tormentors in Jesus' powerful name.

GRASSHOPPERS

Chief Characteristics

In general, grasshoppers are usually green, brown, or olive in color. These insects have antennae and tend to jump from one area to the next.

Unlocking the Dream:
What Do Grasshoppers Represent?

Grasshoppers often symbolize *multitudes to destroy* (Judges 6:5; Numbers 13:33; Judges 7:12; Isaiah 40:22; Amos 7:1; Malachi 3:17).

How to Pray

Ask the Holy Spirit to confuse the network of the enemy. Activate Deuteronomy 28:7, and ask the Lord to

Chapter 9: Human Anatomy & Physiology

let your enemies flee seven ways. Ask the Holy Spirit to strike every demonic grasshopper-like spirit with thunder and lightning bolt. Command them to die in Jesus' name.

LOCUST

Chief Characteristics

These insects normally travel long distances in large groups and can be very destructive or difficult to control. They often wreak havoc on crops or agricultural land.

Unlocking the Dream: What Do Locusts Represent?

Locusts often symbolize *destructive enemies and evil spirits* (Nahum 3:17; Isaiah 33:4; Revelation 9:3, 7).

How to Pray

Command every destructive spirit to die by the fire of God. Declare that no weapon formed against your favor and blessings shall prosper. Ask Jehovah-Jireh to put a permanent hedge around your wealth and industry. Activate Malachi 3, and summon the angels of God to smite the devourer for your sake.

REPTILES

ALIGATOR

Chief Characteristics

These reptiles have tough bodies, v-shaped or pointed snouts, and muscular flat tails. They also have powerful jaws and sharp teeth, which aid them in carrying out vicious attacks. Alligators have the ability to drown and rip their victims in a flash. Still, they are usually found in slow, fresh-moving waters, rivers, and swamps. They also have the ability to spin on the axis of their body with the victim in their mouth, tearing their prey apart if it cannot be swallowed whole.

Real Life Alligator Encounter

A Utah alligator handler, Lindsay, was suddenly drawn into the water in a split second on August 14, 2021, by an alligator named Darth Gator. Lindsay only managed to escape death because of the grace of God. Still, her expert training in dealing with alligators, as well as the help of Donnie, who jumped on the alligator's back out of desperation to save her, proved successful. Miraculously, the incident only resulted in her hand bleeding profusely, receiving a broken thumb, wrist, and tendon damage.

Chapter 9: Human Anatomy & Physiology

Unlocking the Dream: What Do Alligators Represent?

As it is in the natural, so are these reptiles dangerous in the dream world. In light of this, you should now be aware that dreams of alligators in the bad sense must not be taken for a joke, especially when they are attacking. To decode your dream, you must pay keen attention to the setting, the size, and the number of alligators that were present in the dream. By doing so, you will better understand where the spiritual attack is coming from and the severity of the attack. The number of alligators will give you clues as to the networking of the enemy and its strong base. Therefore, dreams about alligators in the bad sense *normally point to damage, death, or destruction of victims.* Notwithstanding, alligator skin is very expensive and normally used to make expensive bags, accessories, and clothing. In the good sense, dreams about alligators could be *connected to wealth*, but this is very rare. Thus, the dreamer must examine the dream within context so as not to be deceived by the enemy.

How to Pray

Ask Jesus Christ—The Good Shepherd—to keep you safe from damage, death, and destruction. Bind every evil alligator spirit that comes to kill or spin away your blessings. Activate the sword of God and ask the Holy Spirit to penetrate their impenetrable bodies. Command water quakes to swallow up every demonic alligator and wipe them out forever.

LIZARD

Chief Characteristics

There are approximately 4,000 species of lizards, and they range in many different sizes and categories. Lizards are either herbivores, omnivores, or carnivores with long bodies and tails. They live in many different habitats, inclusive of trees, on ground, and in rocks.

Unlocking the Dream: What Do Lizards Represent?

Lizards normally represent *uncleanness, ancestral spirit for guarding a family line, divination, magic, secret, and sorcery* (Leviticus 11:29–30).

Dream of Lizard Blocking the Road

This indicates that the forces of darkness are working against your progress, trying to prevent you from accessing God's divine blessings and favor, trying to prevent you from fulfilling your assignments.

How to Pray

Cry out to God and ask Him to strike every destiny blocker with His lightning and thunder.

Ask the Lord to send angelic assistance to remove and destroy every hindrance to your assignments. Command every ancestral spirit to receive the fire of the Almighty God. Ask Jehovah-Gibbor to break you free from every

Chapter 9: Human Anatomy & Physiology

ancestral curse in the mighty name of Jesus. Superimpose or replace every curse with the blessings of the Almighty God.

SNAKES

Chief Characteristics

There are approximately 3,000 species of snake, of which 600 are venomous. Most snakes lay eggs while others give birth to live young. Some snakes live in water while others live on land. Snakes hunt mostly at night. To kill their prey, snakes can give a rapid-fire bite in less than a split second. Snakes' lower jaws can separate from their upper jaws, which gives them the ability to eat prey whole, even up to three times larger than the diameter of their head. The snake's teeth are also special in that they are rear-facing, therefore giving them the ability to hold prey and prevent them from escaping. Interestingly, even after a snake's head is severed, the head still has the power to bite the victim, releasing deadly venom. Snake venom composition varies widely, and some have attributed this to their diet (Pahari et al., 2007).

Unlocking the Dream: What Do Snakes Represent?

Snake dreams usually represent *sorcery, witchcraft, divination, the seduction of the occult, and high-order demonic forces, linked with marine kingdom spirits that come to destroy and kill.*

Specific Types of Snakes and Functions

- *Cobra Snake*: These aggressive snakes are famous for their iconic hoods and their forked tongues. They are the longest of all venomous snakes and are able to raise up to one-third of their body to attack their victims. These snakes are often seen in trees, on land, and in water.

Cobra's Spiritual Function: In spiritual warfare, the cobra spirit comes to mesmerize, seduce, manipulate, alter destiny, mind control and cause broken focus.

- *Python Snake*: These devastating nonvenomous snakes kill their victims by wrapping around them and squeezing them tighter and tighter until they meet their demise. They have the ability to eat their prey whole.

Python's Spiritual Function: These snakes come to create a false burden, overwhelm, exasperate, and swallow up blessings, illegally hold up or hold back assignments and breakthroughs.

- *Boa Constrictor*: Also known as a red tail boa, these nonvenomous snakes only interact when they are mating but otherwise live on their own. They normally bite when they perceive a threat. Boa constrictors are known to lie still and ambush their prey.

Boa's Spiritual Function: This demonic spirit comes to attack suddenly, crush, stifle, strangle, suffocate, and deceive.

- *Anaconda Snake*: These constrictor snakes also prefer to live alone and are mostly found by

Chapter 9: Human Anatomy & Physiology

dark rivers and swamps. They can give birth to live offspring, over twenty-five at a time. From crocodiles to jaguars and even cannibalism, these snakes consume. Their eyes are strategically located high on their head, thus allowing clear vision while their bodies are undetected below water. Similarly, their noses also allow them to breathe while being fully submerged under water, and they rely on stealth to attack prey suddenly.

Anaconda's Spiritual Function: Like the boa constrictor, these snakes come to stifle, strangle, and suffocate.

- *Rattle Snakes:* These venomous snakes have a rattle located on their tails that gives a rattling sound to deter predators or passersby. Their favorite habitats are open areas near rock as well as grassland.

Rattlesnake's Spiritual Function: This diabolical spirit comes to drive fear, confuse, mesmerize, destroy, kill, hunt, plague, and monitor.

How to Pray

Pay keen attention to the type of snake that is in operation and ask the Holy Spirit to destroy its agenda. Sever not just the head but the entire body of the snake or serpentine spirit with the sword of God. Ask Jehovah God to put a hook in the mouth of the serpent and to destroy every marine kingdom spirit. Destroy every snake with the fire of God. Close every door to the enemy with the blood of Jesus and loosen yourself free from every perversion and seduction. Announce that you will not be mesmerized, confused, or consumed by the serpent. Cover your mind, body, soul, and spirit with the blood of Jesus Christ of Nazareth.

CHAPTER 9:
HUMAN ANATOMY & PHYSIOLOGY

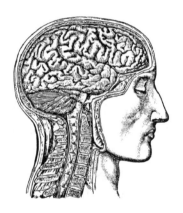

"Each part of the body represents something different. Your feet represent mobility. A dream attack on your feet usually indicates the enemy wants to destroy your authority, dominion or restrict your movement and progress."

Human anatomy mainly concerns the different structures of the human body, while physiology focuses on the function of each structure. The human body is fascinating, and each organ is so uniquely designed to carry out very important tasks. Thus, any disruption of these organs will adversely affect their functions. What if the dream concerning your head was a warning to protect your head from the evil arrows of the enemy? What if dreaming of your eye the other day was telling you to cover your eyes from impending danger? The fact is that the believer is constantly being attacked by the enemy, and so we must be super alert. It is said that "Nobody knows your body better than you do." Well, did you know that your body has many portals of entry that must be protected? Yes, it certainly does. By portal of entry, I mean any areas on our body through which things can enter our tissues or make us susceptible. Some of these portals of entry include our eyes, ears, nose, mouths, broken skin, anus, penis, and vagina. Many people have dreams on a regular basis concerning these portals of entry; this is very significant and requires unlocking. Furthermore, it is important that we cover these portal entries with the blood of Jesus Christ before we go to sleep. A little consecrated olive oil smeared on these areas, backed by prayer, is also effective means of coverage from the darkness of this world. Let's now look even closer at the human body and unlock its meaning in the dream world.

MAN

Chief Characteristics

Man is made in the image of the Almighty God. This constitutes man's intelligence, which is far above all other creatures that God created on planet earth. Man not only knows how to think, but we have the ability to discern between right and wrong, hence possessing a will to make the right choice. We are also blessed with the ability to worship and have daily fellowship with God. Of all the resources available on earth, man represents the highest, greatest, and best.

Unlocking the Dream: What Does Man Represent?

Man generally represents *the image and likeness of God, source, a seed* (Genesis 1:26–28).

DREAM SEEING PASTOR/PRIEST/PROPHETS

Unlocking the Dream

These dreams are very important as a pastor/priest/prophet generally symbolizes *God's mouthpiece or oracle*. Dreams of seeing a pastor, priest, or prophet in the good sense may represent *the Holy Spirit giving you divine instruction or direction*. However, the Bible also speaks of false prophets; therefore, what the pastor, priest, or prophet is doing in the dream is very important as their actions may indicate otherwise. If the pastor, priest, or prophet is attacking you, *it simply means that the enemy is using deception*, and you must be careful not to let down your guard. The fact is the enemy is skillful at using familiar faces (persons you love or are acquainted with) to deceive and launch vicious attacks.

How to Pray

Activate your spiritual senses to come alive and declare that you will not be deceived by the enemy. Declare that you will be at the right place at the right time like Samuel to hear from God. Tell the Holy Spirit that His will is your will, and it is your pleasure to obey Him. Command every God-given gift in your life to come alive and proclaim, "I shall function at my highest capacity and be the best that God desires me to be."

DREAM OF SEEING AN INSANE MAN

Unlocking the Dream

An insane man typically symbolizes *evil or demonic strongmen, demons* (Matthew 8:28–30).

How to Pray

Ask the Redeemer to rescue you from every demonic strongman. Use your authority and power to defeat them by binding the demons, destroying their assignments and purpose. Establish the will of God over and against the plans of the adversary.

Chapter 9: Human Anatomy & Physiology

DREAM OF A MAN RUNNING AFTER YOU

Unlocking the Dream

This normally represents *demonic forces wanting to destroy your God-given purpose and destiny*. It represents a want to restrict and bind you or to hinder your progress, especially if the dream setting is somewhere you previously lived, worked, studied, etc.

How to Pray

You must command every destiny terminator to fall and die in the powerful name of Jesus. You must destroy every destiny blocker or stopper with the fire of God. Command every anti-progressive spirit to die by the consuming fire of the Almighty God.

DREAM OF DEAD MAN/WOMAN

Unlocking the Dream

These dreams generally symbolize *familiar spirits in operation*. Dark Arts practitioners (necromancers, witchcraft workers, etc.) connect with evil spirits to deceive and harm persons by intruding in their dreams. Dreams like these indicate that one's destiny or assignments are under attack.

How to Pray

You must destroy every covenant that was established with you and the deceased, anything that gives these evil spirits a legal right to communicate with you. Declare that any power assigned to waste your destiny be wasted! Declare that you shall not die, but you shall live. Bind every demon of untimely death and render them powerless in Jesus' mighty name. Loosen their hold on your life. Loosen their hold from your destiny in Jesus' mighty name.

DREAM OF MEN IN WHITE "HOODIE" CLOTHING

The Ku Klux Klan or KKK is a group that is well known for committing heinous atrocities. Their outfit consists of wearing white hoodies. A dream of men in hoodies that looks like the Ku Klux Klan must not be taken lightly.

Unlocking the Dream

Dreams of this nature represent *demonic forces coming to harm or kill*. These dreams symbolize *death, destruction, or bad news*.

How to Pray

Take authority and bind every death demon. Bind the strongman of death, destruction, and disappointment. Use your legal right as a child of God. Be vigilant and destroy

Chapter 9: Human Anatomy & Physiology

the plans of the enemy. The Bible says, "You will also decree a thing, and it will be established" (Job 22:28, NKJV). Begin to decree that "No weapon formed against you shall prosper" (Isaiah 54:17, NKJV). Declare that sudden and untimely death is not your portion. Announce that with long life, you shall live and show Christ your salvation (Psalm 91:16). Find every scripture that speaks to life and activate and embrace them today without hesitancy.

DREAM OF SEEING A BABY

Unlocking the Dream: What Does a Baby Represent?

A sweet baby generally symbolizes *birthing, ministry,* or *soul.*

An ugly baby normally symbolizes *demons* or *the demoniacs.*

DREAM OF A BABY IN WATER DROWNING AND YOU REVIVE THE BABY

Unlocking the Dream

This symbolizes *your soul, anointing, and ministries being revived or resurrected.*

DREAM OF GIVING BABY A BATH

Unlocking the Dream

This symbolizes *cleansing, renewal of soul, or ministry/transformation* (Titus 3:5; John 3:3–5).

DREAM OF BABY FECES ALL OVER YOU

Unlocking the Dream

This represents *pollution; the enemy is polluting you in your dream.*

How to Pray

Repent of all filthiness and close every open door to the enemy with the blood of Jesus. Pray aggressive warfare prayers; ask the Holy Spirit to kill every dream polluter. Ask the Holy Spirit to cleanse every area of your life from dream pollution. Say this command, "Every power of pollution in my body, die in the name of Jesus!"

DREAM OF DECEPTIVE TRAVELERS

A dream about a deceptive traveler involves dreaming of someone traveling with you, either going before you or walking behind or alongside you. The person often appears to be good, then suddenly they strike or attack you violently. Sometimes the individual traveling with you

Chapter 9: Human Anatomy & Physiology

appears to be insane or dresses insane, but the intention is to deceive and destroy.

Unlocking the Dream: What Do Deceptive Travelers Represent?

These demonic traveler dreams represent *deception at the highest level*. To unlock dreams of this nature, look carefully at the setting. Can you recognize the location of the dream? For example, in your former community, in a church, at the workplace, etc. If you can identify the setting, you can connect or trace where the attack is coming from.

Another clue to unlock the dream concerns the style or appearance of the demonic, deceptive traveler. What color was the traveler in? How did the traveler look? For example, the traveler was in full black, and his clothes were "pitchy patchy." The color of the clothes and the styles are sometimes clues to the interpretation as well. Why? The scripture says, "God is light; in Him there is no darkness at all" (1 John 1:5, NIV). So, in warfare, evil or sin is normally associated with darkness, devils, and demons. Therefore, an insane or "mad man" dressed in black is a clear indication of darkness. This represents a demonic strongman.

Still, another clue to unlocking this dream concerns where the enemy attacked, that is, your feet, your hand, your head, etc. This is important because each part of the body represents something different. Your feet represent mobility—an attack on your feet indicates the enemy wants to restrict your movement or progress. Your hands represent industry—an attack on your hand indicates that the enemy wants to destroy your industry, finance, creativity, etc. Your head holds your brain, where God releases creative ideas and revelation—an attack on your head indicates that the enemy wants to block the revelatory knowledge that is geared to advance you. In addition, the enemy may want to confuse you and, at worst, destroy you completely since your brain is a delicate organ. The reality is that "if the enemy can defeat you in the mind, the battle has already been won."

Furthermore, did the deceptive traveler manage to cut, stab, shoot, or injure you in the dream? This represents a wound or a blow. Just as if someone stabs you physically and you are wounded, it's the same thing in spiritual warfare. Be vigilant and look out for someone or something trying to hurt you, whether emotionally, financially, or otherwise.

Did you see your blood leak out as a result of the attack? Also, in the dream, sometimes another deceptive person may give you an ointment to rub on the area, and then something leaks out, but you cannot tell if it is blood or something else leaked out. This again is another clue because clearly, the demonic strongman's intentions here would be to cripple you and cause whatever strength, favor, and blessings to leak out.

The Bible teaches us that "the life of a creature is in the blood" (Leviticus 17:11, NIV). So, when the creature's blood leaks out eventually, the creature dies. Clearly, the enemy wants to cause whatever progress in your life to die. The Bible says, "The thief comes only to steal, kill and destroy..." (John 10:10, NIV).

How to Pray

Bind every deceptive demonic traveler strongman. Remember, demons are unclean spirits; they are not physical beings even though they may enter a physical being. So, when you pray, declare, "I bind every demonic strongman that comes to attack my health, my wealth, or my favor, etc."

When praying, bind the deceptive strongman and send them to become the footstool of Jesus Christ. Ephesians 1:22 teaches us that *God has appointed Jesus as head over everything and has placed them under His feet.*

Also, you can ask the Lord of Hosts to release His military angels like Gabriel to chain these deceptive demonic travelers and send them to the pit of hell. For example, say, "O God of Elijah, let Your angel—with like stature of Gabriel—bind these demonic travelers with everlasting chains of fire and cast them into the pit of torment. Lord of Hosts, bind them and send them to the pit of Sheol or the abyss of Hades."

Mark 5 teaches us that we can destroy these demonic forces' works and purpose. We have the authority to destroy their works and to ask Jesus to torment them. In Mark 5:7 (NKJV), the legions of the insane demonic man cried out, "Jesus, Son of the Most High God...I implore You...do not torment me." The word "torment" in the text is the Hebrew word *basanizo (bas-an-id-zo)*, which means "to torture, to be harassed, distressed and pain." Therefore, your prayer should be "O God, torment my tormentor, distress my stressors, harass my harassers, or pursue and judge my pursuer."

Use the blood of Jesus to cleanse any poison or toxin you received from the attack. Ask God to bind up the wound with His precious blood. Ask the Almighty God for a divine blood transfusion. Declare that all contaminants are eradicated by the blood of Jesus. Say, "I flush out my body, my organs, systems, and my cells with the blood of Jesus. I neutralize every contaminant in my body with the blood of Jesus."

DREAM OF PEOPLE FROM A FORMER COMMUNITY

Many people dream of returning to their communities and eating from familiar faces. Some receive dreams of even eating from the deceased. These evil attacks need to be destroyed immediately by the fire of God.

Unlocking the Dream: What Does a Former Community Represent?

This is an indication that the enemy has some legal access to feed you. Some covenant was established between

Chapter 9: Human Anatomy & Physiology

you and your former community. In an attempt to help their children, many times, parents go about it the wrong way and establish a covenant with the dark world without even being aware. Many people's navel strings have been planted in communities that are cursed, and hence, an anti-progressive spirit is legally operating against them. Every time a major breakthrough occurs, something drastically happens to prevent it from manifesting. Many times, forefathers have gone to witchcraft workers and offered food, etc., to idols.

How to Pray

To destroy this type of dream, the individual needs to confess personal sin as well as the sin of the previous generations. The individual needs to renounce every tie/soul tie and break it by the fire of the Most High God. The person needs to establish a new covenant with the Holy Spirit and superimpose blessings over every curse. The individual must ask the Holy Spirit to cleanse their system with the blood of Jesus Christ. Also, you can anoint your mouth with consecrated olive oil, seal it with the blood of Jesus, and ask the Holy Spirit to prevent any contaminating spirit from having access to feed you in your sleep.

HAIR

Chief Characteristics

One of the chief characteristic features of mammals is hair. Functions of the hair include the protection against external factors, producing apocrine sweat and pheromones, impact on social and sexual interactions, and being a resource for stem cells. The two most distinctive parts of the hair are the follicle and the hair shaft. The follicle is located under the skin and is the living part of the hair. It is responsible for the generation of hair. On the other hand, the hair shaft is the non-living part of the hair that is mostly seen at or above the skin surface. Thus, it is not anchored to the follicle. Notably, humans have around five million hair follicles, of which 100,000 are located on the scalps (Erdogan, 2017).

Unlocking the Dream: What Does Hair Represent?

The Hebrew word *nezer* (*neh-zer*) is used for "hair," and it refers to "something set apart; dedication of a priest or Nazarite, hence, unshorn locks; a chaplet of royalty; consecration, crown, separation." In contrast, the Greek word *Thrix* (*threeks*) is used to refer to "hair of beast or man." It is used to signify the smallest detail, which shows the exceeding care and protection bestowed by God upon His children (Matthew 10:30; Luke 21:18; Luke 12:7, 21, 18) (Strong, 2001).

Chapter 9: Human Anatomy & Physiology

To interpret these dreams, you must pay attention to the conditions or characteristics of the hair. For example, its color, length, or strength.

Hair represents "health and beauty in youth; wisdom and vitality in old age" (Proverbs 16:31, Matthew 10:30, Luke 12:7).

Long hair may represent glory for women but dishonor for men, disheveled or loose hair can also mean dishonor (1 Corinthians 11:14–15).

Your hair also symbolizes your anointing as well as covering.

DREAM OF SOMEONE CUTTING YOUR HAIR

Unlocking the Dream

This represents your anointing, strength, or glory is being attacked or tampered with. You must pray aggressive prayers for its renewal or restoration. Command every destiny killer and glory snatcher to be destroyed by the fire of God. Ask the Holy Spirit to restore your anointing (Judges 16).

DREAM OF SOMEONE COMBING YOUR HAIR

Unlocking the Dream

Depending on the context, this can signify your anointing is being renewed, strengthened, and protected.

HEAD

Chief Characteristic

The head refers to the part of the body that contains the eyes, ears, mouth, nose, and brain.

The Hebrew word *Qodqod* (*kod-kode*) is used for head, and it means "the crown of the head, top of the head, pate, and scalp." Another Hebrew word used is *Ro-sh* (*roshe*), which means "chief, beginning, top, captain, rulers, excellent." In contrast, the Greek word *kephale* is used for head, and it refers to "the sense of seizing; the most readily taken hold of" (Strong, 2001).

Unlocking the Dream: What Does the Head Represent?

Consequently, the head symbolizes *the center of life and the cornerstone of one's existence, the seat of energy, and the active principle of the whole individual*. It represents the entire body and the focal point for receiving blessings (Proverbs 10:6).

Dream of Receiving a Shot in the Head

One lady reported that she dreamt of being shot in the head by a man, and after waking up, the area where she got the shot felt tender.

Chapter 9: Human Anatomy & Physiology

Unlocking the Dream

What really happened is that she received a diabolic bullet in her dream. This vicious demonic attack clearly was intent on killing or destroying her. As it is in the natural, so it is in the spiritual. Guns and gunshots must not be taken lightly, especially when they are directed toward the head. These evil bullets are launched to destroy an individual's life and the focal point for receiving blessings.

How to Pray

The dreamer must arise and pray against the harmful effect of every diabolic bullet. The dreamer must ask the Holy Spirit to cover their head on the day of battle. The apostle Paul says, "Put on the whole armour of God..." (Ephesians 6:11–18, KJV). The dreamer must apply the blood of Jesus to the head and ask the Lord to heal the head and realign any area that was misaligned as a result of the bullet. In addition, ask the Holy Spirit to cover every area of your finance so that demonic forces will not be able to cause your finance to leak out as a result of sickness attacks.

DREAM OF SOMEONE POURING OINTMENT ON YOUR HEAD

Unlocking the Dream

In the good sense, it represents being anointed or designated for a purpose. It also symbolizes another level, promotion, kingship, and healing (1 Samuel 16:13; James 5:14).

In the bad sense, it represents being desecrated or tampering with your anointing, purpose, assignment, office, and blessing.

Tips

1. Be careful of who lays their hands on your head, especially during prayer. This is one of the easiest ways evil transferences occur as well as the diminishing of your anointing.
2. When you are experiencing spiritual warfare, you may need to anoint your head with consecrated oil and make daily declarations, for example, "Cover my head with Your blood, Jesus. Adonai-Lord, [cover] my head in the day of battle" (Psalm 140:7, NKJV).
3. Also, the Holy Spirit sometimes may direct you to cover your head with a cloth (for example, a prayer shawl) when you are going to bed. This is strategic as it prevents your head from being attacked, so I implore you to obey Him.

THE BRAIN

Chief Characteristics

The brain is made of more than one hundred billion nerves and is one of the largest organs in the human body. It contains a cranium (skull) that helps to protect it from injuries. Notably, the brain can be negatively affected

Chapter 9: Human Anatomy & Physiology

by many different issues, including strokes, headaches, concussions, brain tumors, meningitis, dementia, Alzheimer's disease, Parkinson's disease, Huntington's disease, epilepsy, brain abscess, intracerebral hemorrhage, etc. (Hoffman, 2021).

Different Parts of the Brain

- *The Brain Stem*: responsible for breathing and sleep control
- *The Hippocampus*: Responsible for encoding new memories. Deals with normal recognition memory as well as spatial memory (when the memory tasks are like recall tests).
- *The Amygdala:* The amygdala helps determine what memories to store, and it plays a part in determining where the memories are stored based on whether we have a strong or weak emotional response to the event. Its main job is to regulate emotions, such as fear and aggression (fear memories). The amygdala is involved in memory consolidation, the process of transferring new learning into long-term memory. The amygdala seems to facilitate encoding memories at a deeper level when the event is emotionally arousing.
- *The Prefrontal Cortex*: plays a role in remembering semantic tasks
- *The Cerebellum*: is the largest part of the hindbrain and plays the role of processing procedural memories, such as how to play the piano. It is also in charge of muscle tone, posture, coordination, and balance. Therefore,

the dysfunction of the cerebellum may result in difficulty in talking, eating, sleeping, and coordinating muscular activity (Singh, 2020).
- *Neurotransmitters*: dopamine, epinephrine, serotonin, glutamate, and acetylcholine; they are involved with the process of memory.
- *The Frontal Lobes*: Deal with motor functions, problem-solving, and judgment.
- *The Parietal Lobes*: Deal with body position, handwriting, and sensation.
- *The Temporal Lobes*: Deal with hearing and memory.
- *The Occipital Lobes*: Deal with the brain's visual processing system.

All in all, the three main brain areas that play significant roles in the processing and storage of different types of memories are the *cerebellum, hippocampus, and amygdala*.

How to Pray

It is important for the dreamer and intercessors to cover the different areas of the brain with the blood of Jesus. Many times, the dreamer complains of not being able to remember their dreams. It is possible that the enemy is attacking your brain. Therefore, you need to pray strategically and cover the different areas of your brain. Furthermore, command every dream snatcher and killer to fall and die in the mighty name of Jesus!

Declare that there shall be no miscommunication in

your brain; instead, your brain shall function according to how God designed and designated it to function. Back it up with the Word of God, "No weapon formed against my brain shall prosper" (Isaiah 54:17).

EYE

Chief Characteristics

The human eye is a fascinating organ and is considered to be the window to the soul by which light enters the body. By looking in a person's eye, we can assess what the person is thinking and feeling. Notably, the eye can be divided into three main sections, namely, the outer layer, the middle layer, and the inner layer. The outer eye consists of the sclera (the white area) and the cornea (the transparent part that covers the pupil and iris). The middle eye consists of the iris (the colorful part), pupil, lens, ciliary body, and choroid. Still, the inner eye consists of the retina, rods, cones, optic disc, and optic nerve (Salazar et al., 2018).

Unlocking the Dream: What Do Eyes Represent?

Eyes generally symbolize *sight, insight, and foresight* (Psalm 66:7; Proverbs 16:2, 30; Matthew 6:22–23; Revelation 4:6).

You must pay keen attention to the eyes in the dream. Pay keen attention to the color of the eyes. A red eye symbolizes demons. A staring eye symbolizes hatred, animosity, and destruction.

A dream of someone attacking your eyes and a dream of seeing lewdness or indecent exposure are serious dreams that should not be taken lightly. Here, the enemy is trying to impair your vision, especially if you operate with a prophetic gift. The evil spirit may also be trying to entice you or lure you into a particular lifestyle (perversion). When the eye is being attacked in the dream, this can result in eye sickness, whether physical or spiritual.

How to Pray

Study the different parts of the eyes (retina, sclera, optic disc, optic nerves, etc.) and pray a prayer of coverage over the different eye parts. Ask the Holy Spirit to cleanse your eyes off every contamination. Avoid things that contaminate your eyes in a natural way so as not to give the enemy the legal right to afflict you in your dream (e.g., porn). Ask the Holy Spirit to burn off every scale from your eyes. Pray scriptures that deal with healing to superimpose health and healing over your eyes rather than sickness and disease. Anoint your eyes with consecrated olive oil before going to your bed and declare that your eyes are covered with the blood of Jesus.

EARS

Chief Characteristics

This essential organ is responsible for hearing and balance and is essential for effective communication. It allows us to understand our environment as well as alert us of impending danger. Similar to the eye, our ear has three major sections. They are the outer, middle, and inner ear. The outer ear performs the role of capturing sound from the environment, which travels to the middle and inner ear for us to hear. The outer ear consists of the pinna (the outer side part of the ear) and the external auditory canal or tube. The middle ear consists of the tympanic cavity and ossicles. Notably, the tympanic membrane (eardrum) divides the middle ear from the external ear. Still, the inner ear consists of the cochlea, vestibule (for balance), and semicircular canals (Alper et al., 2017).

Unlocking the Dream: What Do Ears Represent?

The Hebrew word for ears is *Ozen*, and it means "broadness, advertise, audience, displeased, reveal, show." The ear generally represents "to pay attention, to listen, to inform, spiritual hearing for understanding." When pierced, it represents perpetual servitude (Genesis 20:8; Exodus 21:6; Matthew 11:15) (Strong, 2001).

DREAM OF SOMEONE POURING OINTMENT IN YOUR EAR

Unlocking the Dream

If your ear is physically sick, in the good sense, it can mean healing; however, in the bad sense, it can represent that your ear gate is being desecrated or coming under attack. Here, the emotions or how you felt while having the dream and even immediately after it are crucial to dissecting dreams of this nature.

DREAM OF YOUR EARS BEING SICK

Unlocking the Dream

This implies that your ear gate needs healing and cleansing. If you don't address this speedily, you may miss important instructions from God, which will negatively affect your assignments.

How to Pray

Ask the Holy Spirit to open up your spiritual ear gate for you to receive supernatural understanding. Ask the Almighty God to cover the different areas of your ear with His precious blood. Pray strategically by calling each area of your ears (ear canal, ear pinna, organs of balance, malleus (hammer), incus (anvil), eardrum, etc.). Consecrate your ears with consecrated olive oil and seal them with the blood of Jesus.

NOSE

Chief Characteristics

The nose is a part of the respiratory system. In other words, it helps us to breathe and smell. The nose is divided into two (2) main parts, the nasal cavity and the external nose. The nasal cavity refers to the inside of the nose, which has little hairs to filter the air we breathe as well as block dust and dirt from getting into the lungs. In contrast, the external nose is a pyramidal structure located in the midface with its base on the facial skeleton (Mete & Akbudak, 2018).

With this in mind, the Hebrew word *aph* (*af*) refers to "the nose or nostril, hence, the face, occasionally a person, rapid breathing, anger, passion, longsuffering, countenance, forbearing, forehead, snout" (Strong, 2001).

Unlocking the Dream: What Does the Nose Represent?

The nose helps us to breathe or smell; thus, a metal hook through the nose symbolizes forcing one to obey (Isaiah 37:29; Ezekiel 16:12). Dreams of someone forcing or deceiving you to smell a potion? This indicates that the enemy is trying to "mesmerize or poison you." Inhaling certain harmful chemicals in the natural environment can result in serious harm or injuries. The same is true in the spiritual; hence, not canceling dreams of inhaling substances can result in "sickness inclusive of brain damage, lung damage, mouth problems, stomach problems, and eventually death."

How to Pray

Pray for Jesus' blood coverage of your spiritual senses. Cleanse your system from every poison and toxins with the blood of Jesus. Reverse the curse on the enemy. Make aggressive military-style declarations that sickness and disease must be far from you. Declare that you are healed by the blood of Jesus, the Word of God, and by the power of the Holy Spirit.

MOUTH

Chief Characteristics

The mouth refers to the part of the body that food enters through and contains the teeth, tongue, vestibule, and soft and hard palates. The Hebrew word *Peh* is used for mouth and translates as "the means of blowing; speech; edge; commandment; word; appointment; talk to; mind; entry; portion." The Greek word *stoma* also translates to mouth and means "a gash in the face; language; an opening (in the earth); the front or edge of a weapon" (Strong, 2001).

Unlocking the Dream: What Does the Mouth Represent?

The mouth symbolizes *character and internal emotions* (Proverbs 13:3; Luke 6:45; Ephesians 4:29).

Many people dream of eating in their sleep. This is very strategic as dreams of this nature are aimed at destroying your health and wealth. Many times, people are sick because of eating in their sleep. Sadly, sometimes doctors can't even find what the source of the problem is, so they cannot get a proper diagnosis, and their sickness leads to their demise. The devil and his agents are very vicious.

Chapter 9: Human Anatomy & Physiology

How to Pray

You must use the fire of God to destroy every food that is offered on demonic altars that the enemy is feeding you with. You must call forth angelic hosts to slaughter every night caterer and morning server of evil food and drinks. You must break every covenant that was established between you and the enemy, whether knowingly or unknowingly. You must ask the Lord to arise and let your enemies be scattered by fire and by force.

TEETH

Chief Characteristics

During a lifetime, humans have two sets of teeth, namely, primary teeth and permanent teeth. The primary teeth are first to appear in a child's mouth and are later replaced by permanent teeth. Generally, there is a total of thirty-two permanent teeth. Notably, adults have four types of teeth, namely, molar, premolar, incisors, and canine. Still, there are four main parts to each tooth, namely, the enamel, dentin, pulp, and root (Alshami et al., 2019).

The Hebrew word *Shen* (*Shane*) is used for teeth referring to a tooth as "sharp, ivory, a cliff, sharp, crag, and forefront." In contrast, the Greek *odous* (*Odooce*) means "a tooth; gnashing of teeth" (Job 16:9; Psalm 3:7; Acts 7:54, Matthew 8:12; Mark. 9:18; Luke 13:28) (Strong, 2001).

Unlocking the Dream: What Do Teeth Represent?

Teeth generally symbolize *death, decay, defeat, or danger.* The gnashing of teeth symbolizes intense anger and suffering. Many people have dreams of teeth falling out and often find out that the death of a loved one shortly follows. Others have dreams of tooth decay only to realize their businesses are going down. Still, a great number of people have dreamt of being bitten by insects, animals, and even humans. Whenever this occurs, transference has just taken place, as evil poisons or toxins have been released in the body that must be urgently destroyed by prayer, and failure to do so often proves fatal.

How to Pray

Make an announcement that you or your loved ones shall not die but live. Command every demon of death or spirit attached to untimely death to fall and die in the mighty name of Jesus. Ask the Holy Spirit to reverse every death and every decay to the enemy's camp in the mighty name of Jesus. Use the blood of Jesus for protection and plea over your life, loved ones, and businesses. Activate Psalm 91 and decree, "No evil shall befall me nor shall any plague come near my dwelling in Jesus' name."

Chapter 9: Human Anatomy & Physiology

TONGUE

Chief Characteristics

The tongue is a sensory-motor organ responsible for oral functions, inclusive of speech, swallowing, etc.

Notably, the Hebrew word *Lashown* translates to tongue and means, "An instrument used for licking, eating, or speech; a fork of flame, a cove of water, wedge, babbler, flame, speaker, and talker." *Charash* also is used for tongue, meaning "to scratch, to engrave, work in metal, plow, to fabricate, to devise, to be deaf; dumbness; silence, practice secretly, worker" (Strong, 2021).

The Greek equivalent *Glossa* (*gloce-sah*) is used for tongue, and it translates as "a language; an organ of speech; *phulé*; a tribe, *laos*, a people; *ethos*, a nation." In addition, *Dialektos* is also used for tongue and refers to "a mode of disclosure; dialect; language" (Strong, 2001).

Unlocking the Dream: What Does the Tongue Represent?

The tongue may symbolize a *source of pleasure or source of ill; gossip* (James 3:1–12; Proverbs 18:21).

One of the easiest ways to destroy a person's anointing is through the medium of gossiping. The believer must guard their anointing by refusing to engage in such practices. A dream of someone releasing negative words against you should not be taken lightly. If these dreams are not arrested, they can hinder promotion and, worst case, result in death. That is the reason why the Bible says, "Death and life are in the power of the tongue..." (Proverbs 18:21, KJV).

How to Pray

When praying, you must destroy every false tongue. You must release the sword of God to sever every negative tongue that is working against you. Command every character assassinator to fall and die. Ask the Almighty God to release persons in high places to favor you. Call forth your destiny helper, destiny promoter, and your destiny connectors to locate you speedily.

FACE
Chief Characteristics

The face refers to the front part of the head that possesses the eyes, nose, and mouth. The face consists of both hard and soft tissues. The facial skeleton forms the hard tissue of the face and provides important structural support. At the same time, the soft tissues include the superficial flat compartment, retaining ligament, and mimetic muscles. Other areas include the facial nerves, sensory nerves, and facial arteries (Prendergast, 2012).

Furthermore, the Hebrew word for face is *Paniym* (*paw-neem*), which refers to "the part that turns; presence; sight; countenance [for, against, towards], favor; forefront; the look on one's face; surface or the visible side of something, the front side of something, where the emotions are expressed" (Strong, 2001).

Unlocking the Dream: What Does the Face Represent?

The face represents *image and character of a person* (Exodus 26:9; Genesis 1:2, 17:3; Luke 9:53; Acts 17:26; Revelation 4:7, 10:1).

Whenever you receive a dream concerning the face, to unlock it, you must:

1. Read the countenance: was the face for or against you? Was the face depicting an expression of love or confrontation?
2. Link how you feel while having the dream and seeing the face: fearful, happy, etc.
3. Was the face familiar or strange?

NECK

Chief Characteristics

The neck supports the weight and movement of the head. Its structure includes the anterior, posterior, posterior cervical, and sternocleidomastoid regions (Prendergast, 2012).

Notably, one Hebrew word that translates to "neck" is *gargrowth* (*gar-gher-owth*), and it refers to "the throat." Similarly, the Greek word *Trachelos* (*Trakh-ay-los*) means "the throat, through the idea of mobility; that which holds up the head; life" (Strong, 2001).

Unlocking the Dream: What Does the Neck Represent?

The neck represents *greeting or farewell, stiff-necked, rebellion, or resisting authority* (Genesis 33:4; Acts 20:37; Acts 7:51). Many people wake up out of a dream with scratches all over their necks. Others dream of someone trying to choke them. This dream implies the enemy wants to restrict your mobility. The enemy comes to kill, steal, and destroy. Do not take these dreams simply. Waking up with scratches on any part of the body is an indication of high-order demonic forces attacking you in your sleep. Many times, the enemy will place evil marks as a sign of destruction for the person never to prosper and always be coming under severe witchcraft attacks. Do not allow lack of knowledge to cause you to perish; arise and wage holy war against the devil and his agents.

How to Pray

A victor triumphs over his enemy by placing his foot on the enemy's neck. Cry out to the Holy Spirit and ask Him to give you the enemy's neck and show no mercy (Psalm 18:40). Use the blood of Jesus to wipe out every diabolic mark that comes to hinder you from prospering. Superimpose God's blessings and favor to replace every curse in the mighty name of Jesus. Tell the Lord to turn the way of the wicked upside down. Ask the Holy Spirit to speedily break the hold of the enemy from off your neck.

Chapter 9: Human Anatomy & Physiology

THE SHOULDER

Chief Characteristics

The shoulder is the most mobile joint in the body, used to lift, throw, and push. Its structure consists of three main bones, the humerus (the end of the upper arm bone), the scapula (or shoulder blade), and the clavicle (collarbone). Still, the acromioclavicular joint and the glenohumeral joint are responsible for the movements in our shoulders. Other areas include the acromion, rotator cuff, and cartilage (University of Rochester Medical Center, 2022a.).

The Hebrew word *shkem* (*shek-em*) is used for the shoulder, and it refers to "the neck between the shoulders, the place of burdens. Figuratively, the spur of a hill; back; consent; and portion." Another is *Zrowa* (*zer-o-ah*), meaning "the arm (as stretched out) or the animal foreleg; force; power; mighty strength." Also, *Katheph* (*kaw-thafe*) means "upper end of the arm; lateral projection of anything" (Strong, 2001).

Unlocking the Dream: What Does the Shoulder Represent?

The shoulder generally symbolizes greater power and authority, greater strength (Isaiah 9:6; Luke 15:5).

Dreams of a person giving you a load to carry on your shoulder signify the enemy wants to weaken your power, authority, and strength. The key to unlocking dreams of this nature involves also examining what is being placed upon the shoulder. How did you feel when the load was placed on your shoulder?

How to Pray

Ask the Lord to destroy every false burden and to replace them with His Shalom—peace. Activate Psalm 125:3 and ask the Holy Spirit to destroy every diabolical yoke that comes to weaken you. Activate Jeremiah 51:20 and ask the Holy Spirit to use you as His battle-ax and His weapon of war to destroy demonic kingdoms. Declare that the Lord is the strength of your life, and your authority will not leak out in Jesus' name. Ask the Holy Spirit to re-baptize you with His Dunamis—miraculous—prevailing supernatural power and passion.

ARM

Chief Characteristics

The arm refers to the part between the shoulder and the wrist.

Unlocking the Dream: What Does the Arm Represent?

The arm normally symbolizes God's power and authority (Luke 1:51, 12:38).

Dreams of someone injecting your arm or performing surgery on your arm must not be taken as a joke. Here's why: diabolic injections in the dream often cause toxins or poisons to be released in the body, which may result in serious sicknesses as well as physical amputation of the arm or even death. Many times, these evil injections and surgeries cause the dreamer's passion to drain out. Thus, the dreamer finds it most difficult to effectively perform their God-given tasks or assignments.

However, there are times when individuals become sick and receive a divine visitation from God in their dream, and supernatural healing occurs. Discernment is very important in unlocking their dream to determine whether the person is being attacked by the deceptive devil or being helped by God. One tip to make the distinction is that after waking up once it is a divine visitation, the person will feel healed and renewed as opposed to feeling weak, troubled, or weary. Having the feeling of weariness or being troubled is an indication that the devil is on the attack, so urgent prayers need to be set in motion to cancel and sever the plans of the enemy.

How to Pray

Activate Jeremiah 17:14 and cry out to God to heal you, and you shall be healed. Command every diabolical nurse to fall and die. Ask sweet Jesus to flush out every contamination and pollution out of your blood, bones, and tissues in His mighty name. Cancel every sickness and send back every blow to the sender in Jesus' mighty name. Summon God's holy angels of healing to locate you now in Jesus' name. Decree that you shall not die but live healthy, strong, and full of passion and vigor. Establish that your assignments will not be aborted in Jesus' mighty name.

THE HAND

Chief Characteristics

The human hand is one of the essential body parts and enables humans to perform basic daily activities ranging from hand gestures to object manipulation (wave, grip, pull, push, pinch, grasp, handle, etc.). Notably, the hand is located at the end of the arm and is made up of different bones, muscles, and ligaments. There are three main bones found in the hand; these are the phalanges, the metacarpal bones, and the carpal bones. The phalanges refer to the fourteen bones that are found in the fingers of each hand. The metacarpal refers to the five bones that comprise the middle of the hand. Meanwhile, the carpal bones refer to the eight bones that create the wrist (Serrezuela et al., 2020).

Unlocking the Dream: What Does the Hand Represent?

The hand often symbolizes *the work a person does, industry, skill, and a reflection of the will and wishes of the individual*. The left hand symbolizes judgment, while the right hand symbolizes blessings, strength, and promotion (Psalm 118:16; Matthew 25:33, 34; Matthew 25:33; Ecclesiastes 9:10; Colossians 3:23).

Chapter 9: Human Anatomy & Physiology

What do you use your hands to do? This is key to interpreting these dreams.

A dream of anything biting your hand needs to be canceled immediately; the enemy wants to destroy your industry. Biting dreams can also represent satanic incision and identification marks that render the person open for future attacks.

Dreams of using your hands to pay out money must be discerned immediately. In the good sense, it may represent a bountiful harvest. In contrast, in the bad sense, it normally represents evil forces attacking your finances or trying to rob you of your inheritance.

FINGERS

Unlocking the Dream: What Do Fingers Represent?

The finger normally signifies *authority, mercy, grace, judgment, power, and influence*. It also symbolizes the source of deliberate activity of the character of their owners.

To unlock dreams about fingers, ask the following questions: what was the finger writing or doing? How did the fingers look? How did you feel when you were having the dream? How many fingers were there?

How to Pray

Command every evil finger to be destroyed by the fire of God. Use the hammer of God to break every diabolic finger that is restricting your favor and breakthrough into irreplaceable pieces. Ask the Holy Spirit to use His sword to cut every evil hand asunder from your industry, family, and assignments in Jesus' name. Nullify every evil writing against your life with the blood of Jesus Christ. Decree that you will repossess your possessions now in Jesus' name. Cry out like Jabez did, asking the Lord to keep His hand upon you so that the enemy cannot and will not be able to harm you (1 Chronicles 4:10). Command everything that was stolen from your life by evil powers to return a hundredfold in Jesus' name. Ask the Holy Spirit to expose every evil power that's trying to deceive you in your dream to rob you of your wealth. Command every affliction of your finances to die in Jesus' name.

THE HEART
Chief Characteristics

The heart is a special muscle that is responsible for pumping blood around the body. The adult human heart is about the size of a fist and is located two-thirds to the left and one-third to the right of the midline of the thorax, between the two lungs (Cismaru et al., 2017). In other words, the heart is almost in the center of the chest. It beats around eighty times a minute, 115,000 times per day, or about forty-two million times per year. It consists of four chambers, two atria and two ventricles. The atria receive blood coming to the heart while the ventricles pump blood out of the heart. The heart also contains four valves and works with a network of arteries (University of Rochester Medical Center, 2022).

The Hebrew word *lebab* (*lay-bawb*) is used for heart, and it means, "The most interior organ, to consider mind, understanding, comfortable, courage." Another word is *Nephesh*, which means, "A breathing creature, vitality, soul, life, person, mind, desire, appetite." Still, *Leb* (*labe*) is also used, which refers to "the feelings, will, the intellect, the center of anything, mind, understanding, friendly, comfortable." In contrast, the Greek word *Psuche* (*psoo-khay*) translates to "soul/heart." The heart is the "soul/inner man, the seat of desire, the seat of emotions, seat of knowledge and wisdom." Memory is the activity of the heart (Strong, 2001).

Unlocking the Dream: What Does the Heart Represent?

The heart generally symbolizes *the fountain of man's deed as well as the seat of rebellion and pride*. It also represents *the personality, intellect, memory, emotions, desires, will, and center of what we do* (Genesis 8:21; Genesis 6:5; Deuteronomy 6:5; Job 38:36; Psalm 103:1; Psalm 24:4; Colossians 3:23; Exodus 8: 32; Genesis 20:5, Isaiah 38:3; Deuteronomy 8:5; 1 Kings 3:9; Job 22:22).

How to Pray

Cover your heart with the blood of Jesus. Decree and declare that you have the mind of Christ.

Announce that you are emotionally and intellectually stable. Decree and declare that you will only embrace godly desires. Ask the Lord to guard your heart against all hatred, malice, wickedness, perverseness, and unforgiveness. Ask sweet Jesus to let His blood flow through every area of your heart and protect you from every heart attack. Ask the Lord to cover your aorta, pulmonary artery, pulmonary veins, and left and right atrium under His blood.

Ask the Heavenly Father to cover your left and right ventricle, pulmonary valve, aortic valve, tricuspid valve, mitral valve, papillary muscle, superior vena cava, inferior vena cava, ventricular septum, and orifices of coronary arteries under His blood.

THIGH/HIP

Chief Characteristics

Thigh and hip are sometimes used interchangeably in scripture. However, by way of anatomy and physiology, the thigh refers to the lower limb/leg of a human located between the hip and the knee. In contrast, the hip is the area above the leg that is used to support the upper body because of its high level of stability. The hip is a stable ball-and-socket joint that is very flexible and allows for a great range of motion. The hip is a joint formed by the ball-shaped head of the femur and the socket of the pelvis. Notably, the femurs represent the longest and strongest bones in the human body and extend from the hip to the knee (Sarvi, 2018).

Unlocking the Dream: What Does the Thigh/Hip Represent?

The key to unlocking dreams concerning hip/thigh rest is the setting and how the dream impacted or made the dreamer feel. Dreams with thigh/hip, in the good sense, normally symbolize *favor, the choicest part, strength, and mobility* (Genesis 32:32). Conversely, or in the negative sense, they may indicate s*eduction*, especially if the person was exposing the leg/thigh to entice or lure the dreamer. If the dreamer dreamt of being served the hip/thigh of any meat kind, they must properly dissect the dream as it could mean one of two things. In the positive sense, it may indicate favor, but in a negative sense, it may indicate deception and manipulation by the enemy to harm or promote sickness.

How to Pray

Call/summon the angels of breakthrough to release your breakthrough. Command every strongman assigned to your life that is hindering your progress to die speedily in the name of Jesus! Command every power hindering your greatness to die in the name of Jesus. Loosen the favor of God upon your life and your loved ones in Jesus' mighty name.

KNEE

Chief Characteristics

The human knee joint is a complex mechanical structure. It connects the two major bones of the lower limbs together, the femur and the tibia. During daily activities, such as walking and running, a normal knee experiences minimum frictions or wear because of the internal design or structure of the knee. As a matter of fact, apart from its hydrated soft tissues (femoral/tibia cartilages), which facilitate movement, the knee is also properly lubricated by the synovial fluid (Li & Kazemi, 2012).

Unlocking the Dream: What Does the Knee Represent?

The knee generally represents *humility and reverence* (Philippians 2:10–11; Romans 14:11; Ephesians 3:14).

Dreams of bending knees represent paying homage or reverence to whomever the dreamer was bending to. A bending knee also indicates submission.

How to Pray

Decree and declare that you will bow to no other gods but the Almighty God. Legislate/enforce that you will not submit to any evil powers. Announce that no other spirit shall rule over your life except the Spirit of the Living

God. Command diabolical forces to scatter in Jesus' mighty name.

THE FEET

Chief Characteristics

The human feet are fascinating as each foot contains twenty-six bones, thirty-three joints, and over a hundred muscles, tendons, and ligaments. All these work together to provide the body with support, balance, and mobility. The foot is structurally divided into three main parts, namely, the hind foot, midfoot, and forefoot. The hind foot has three joints and connects the midfoot to the ankle. It causes the foot to move up and down as well as slightly turn. The midfoot has five irregular-shaped tarsal bones, which act as shock absorbers. The forefoot has five phalanges of toes and their long connecting bones called metatarsals (Yoon et al., 2011).

Unlocking the Dream: What Do Feet Represent?

The feet normally symbolize *mobility, authority, dominion, and progress.* In contrast, legs generally represent *strength* (Psalm 18:29; Joshua 1:3; John 19:31–34; Hebrews 12:1–2).

A dream of anything attacking your feet is a warning of impending danger as these dreams usually indicate that the enemy wants to destroy your progress, authority, dominion, or restrict your mobility.

"TOE" DREAM ENCOUNTER

In 2020, a lady in Toronto, Canada, reported dreaming of her big toe being cut off. She outlined that she was crying in the dream. She later awoke in a state of great distress. It felt so real; she could not believe it was only a dream because, in the natural, she felt a severe loss. Significantly, immediately after she awoke, she felt an urgent need to pray.

Unlocking the Dream: What Do Toes Represent?

The toe generally symbolizes *destination and stability in power*. However, dreaming of your toe or big toe being severed or dropping off represents "a warning of imminent danger, death, immobility, cutting short one's destiny."

It was a good thing that the lady had been keen to obey God and prayed immediately after she awoke from the dream. Why? If she didn't exercise wisdom, she would today be bemoaning the untimely death of her grandson. The woman of God would later in the day receive an urgent call from a daughter that her grandson, who was perfectly fine, all of a sudden, could not breathe. His body was lifeless, his eyes were rolled over, the color of his skin was turning blue, and his body temperature was as cold as ice. Her grandson was viciously attacked by the powers of darkness. He was gone. What saved him? What brought him back to life? The effectual fervent prayer applied after unlocking the dream. Glory to God! We *must* pay keen attention to our dreams.

How to Pray

Command any satanic dream against your life to backfire in the mighty name of Jesus. Command any demonic forces trying to restrict your movement to fall and die in Jesus' name. Decree and declare any forces formed against your authority to scatter in the mighty name of Jesus. Activate Psalm 18:29 (KJV), "For by thee I will run through a troop; and by my God I will leap over a wall."

Activate *Joshua 1:3 and announce, "Everywhere the sole of my feet touches, I shall have dominion."* Declare every witchcraft instruction against your life to die in the mighty name of Jesus. Command every attack in your dream to backfire in the name of Jesus.

Break yourself free from every untimely death curse in Jesus' powerful name. Send back every death curse to the sender by a hundredfold. Tell the death demons to go back and torment your tormentors in Jesus' name. Release life over everything that concerns you. Announce that you shall not die but live to declare the works of the Lord.

CHAPTER 10:
ELEMENTS OF THE WATERS

"Dreams involving waters normally gear toward destroying destinies, disrupting relationships, depleting anointing, marring character and reputation, implanting illnesses, and destroying finances."

Have you ever dreamt of catching fish or swimming in a boisterous sea? What about standing near a river and communicating with mermaids? These dreams may sound like fairytales, but many people who are experiencing spiritual warfare are often bombarded by elements of the water. Clean and beautiful waters normally are connected with good; however, dirty water dreams frequently indicate some form of turbulence, disaster, or contention ahead. Spiritual warfare dreams involving waters are often linked to certain illnesses which cause severe digestive problems, which often manifest in the swelling of the abdomen, experiencing excessive pain, and other sicknesses that sometimes baffle doctors to diagnose.

Those who are skillful warfare practitioners will tell you about the marine kingdom and the host of wickedness connected to it, where satanic agents attack from the different water bodies. Dreams involving waters normally gear toward destroying destinies, disrupting marriages/relationships, depleting anointing, marring character and reputation, implanting illnesses, and destroying finances. Dreams involving frequent swimming or crossing water bodies and craving for sexual intercourse, especially at specific times (for example, during the full moon), can also be linked to attacks from demonic forces operating from the waters.

DREAM ENCOUNTERS

A young man once shared with me that he was dreaming of making love to a beautiful woman who came from out of the water. The client said she was the most beautiful woman he had ever seen and the best sexual encounter he had experienced. Upon waking up, there was also physical evidence of the encounter (discharge). At the time, he was very happy about the dream and wished to have it again. Wow! Many people like this young man are enjoying these types of dreams, not knowing the devastating effects they can have on their lives. No wonder the Bible teaches that people are destroyed because of a lack of knowledge (Hosea 4:6).

Another individual explained having a dream involving attending a banquet under the water. There was plenty of delicious food, and the person explained that he had a sumptuous feast.

Unlocking the Dream: What Do Water Dreams Represent?

These dreams represent satanic forces attacking from the waters. Eating in our dreams is frequently linked to eating foods offered on demonic altars, which *creates demonic covenants and releases ungodly curses in people's lives.*

Whether you believe it or not, there are several scriptures that address the powers of darkness operating from the waters.

Revelation 12:12 (NKJV) says, "Therefore rejoice, O heavens, and you who dwell in them! Woe to the inhabitants of the earth and the sea! For the devil has come down to you, having great wrath, because he knows his time is short."

Still, the Book of Ezekiel records the prophecy against Pharaoh and Egypt with mention being made of great dragons in the sea (Ezekiel 29:2–3). Likewise, the Book of Isaiah reveals Leviathan, the fleeing and twisted serpent located in the sea (Isaiah 27:1). Yes, the enemy's devices are strategically set. He not only attacks from air and land, but he also attacks from the water bodies.

WATER CREATURES

Chief Characteristics of Leviathan/Sea Monster

The Hebrew word *Leviathan* means a wreathed animal, a serpent, a crocodile, or some other large sea monster, a constellation of the dragon, a symbol of Babylon, and mourning.

The Bible teaches that Leviathan is a piercing serpent (it makes a hiss); a sea monster or dragon in the sea which is full of pride and arrogance (Job 41:33–34; Isaiah 27:1).

Unlocking the Dream: What Does Leviathan Represent?

Dreams involving this crocodile-looking sea creature or monster normally indicate "warfare or high-order demonic forces operating from the marine/sea kingdom." This evil spirit is stubborn, piercing, fierce, and crooked. It comes to drive fear in people as well as to distort, twist, and kill. As a matter of fact, warfare strategists will tell you that the Leviathan spirit comes to destroy relationships by sowing seeds of discord. When this spirit is in operation, it promotes false accusations and thwarts the truth.

Chapter 10: Elements of the Waters

How to Pray

Use the blood of Jesus to cover yourself and your loved ones from every evil element from the water. Ask the Holy Spirit to annihilate every water creature that is waging war against you. Use the Word of God to render powerless every diabolic creature operating from the waters. Shatter and break every attack of the enemies from the waters and render them ineffective in Jesus' mighty name.

FISH

Chief Characteristics

Fishes are cold-blooded vertebrates that live in both salt and fresh water. River fishes consist of species with different body shapes, physiological traits, and swimming styles (Jones et al., 2020).

These animals normally have gills, fins, and scales and breathe by taking water into their mouths.

Unlocking the Dream: What Do Fish Represent?

In many cultures, people interpret dreams of fish to mean pregnancy. Notwithstanding, biblically, fish symbolizes *the souls of men, clean or unclean* (Matthew 4:19; Ezekiel 47:9–10).

Dreams involving fish must be viewed within context. Whereas dreaming of catching fish may represent souls being saved, evangelism, or ministry, dreams of eating fish in spiritual warfare mean something totally different. Witches often feed people fish in their sleep to weaken their spiritual life and cause strange sicknesses in their bodies. After eating fish in their dreams, many people find their Bible reading and prayer life passion dwindled or destroyed. Yes, you have just been fed with unclean food offered on demonic altars. Dreams of this nature need urgent prayer to break the curse.

How to Pray

Ask the Holy Spirit to destroy every demonic fish that is waging war against you. Ask Jehovah-Rapha to purge your body of every contamination. Command every evil night caterer and evil morning server to die by God's fire. Use the Word of God and speak health and healing over your body in the powerful name of Jesus.

FROG/TOAD

Chief Characteristics

Frogs are tailless amphibians with bulging eyes and smooth skin and travel by leaping from one area to the next. They often live in water, on land, or in trees. Their skin may blend in with their environment or even change color. They are distinct from toads, which have rough skins and tend to squat and hop. Also, toads carry poisonous secreting glands on their backs that can paralyze or kill other animals.

Chapter 10: Elements of the Waters

Unlocking the Dream: What Do Frogs/Toads Represent?

Frog dreams normally symbolize "evil spirits, demons, uncleanness" (Exodus 8:1–15; Psalm 78:45; Revelation 16:13). Similarly, a toad is normally linked to witchcraft and occult practices.

How to Pray

Rebuke every unclean spirit and ask the Holy Spirit to cage them for judgment. Command every evil witchcraft power to be rendered powerless and neutralize every poisonous toxin with the blood of Jesus.

MERMAID

Chief Characteristics

Many scholars suggest that mermaids are ancient myths depicting a fishtail female-looking sea goddess with a seductive nature. Nevertheless, as mentioned before, the enemy uses anything that is available to be used to carry out his evil functions. Whether you believe it or not, people have encountered this water creature in real life and have even given graphic details.

Real Life Encounter

One of my chief intercessors told the story of her former partner, who usually goes crab hunting. One day, she advised him not to go, but he refused and still went with his friend. Upon reaching the location, his colleague stayed near the shallow surface, but he went deep diving. What happened next was mind-blowing. Her ex-husband described being greeted by mermaids who insisted on him staying with them under the water. After a while, his friend became worried because the intercessor's ex-husband was not returning. He reported that he suddenly became weak and was unable to move from the position he was in because he rejected the mermaids' offer of staying with them and making love. Thank God for his colleague who decided to dive into the water to see what was hindering him from returning to the surface. It was only then that the mermaids abandoned their wicked intention of drowning.

Unlocking the Dream

Mermaids are demonic water spirits that most times work to seduce people, to carry out illicit sexual activities that entrap their victims. They also frequently make attempts to feed their prey with the aim of destroying their lives. Dreams involving mermaids normally point to the establishment of evil covenants and diabolic initiations to the kingdom of darkness. These wicked covenants and initiations always bring curses and severe disasters to the dreamer, including relationship failure, health issues, and financial hardship.

Chapter 10: Elements of the Waters

SHARKS

Chief Characteristics

Some scientists believe sharks' first appearance dates back to over 455 million years ago. Sharks have excellent vision, especially during the nights. As a matter of fact, their eyeball structure (tapetum) allows them to see with little light. These sea creatures' colors are normally grayish, brown, olive, and blue. Some sharks have pointed teeth (e.g., mako sharks), while others have triangular serrated teeth (e.g., white sharks). Still, the design of their teeth leaves a unique mark upon the prey when they are captured. Reports of unprovoked shark bites on humans have increased by approximately 80 percent globally over the past two decades. White sharks, tiger sharks, and bull sharks are the three main species considered most dangerous to humans (Tate et al., 2019).

Unlocking the Dream: What Do Sharks Represent?

Dreamt of a shark surrounding you, chasing you, or attacking you? Well, unlike a dog, who is considered to be "a man's best friend," not so with a shark. Everyone should be aware that if you are at the beach and see a shark whilst in the water, you would be most blessed to exit alive as sharks come to swiftly kill and destroy.

Dreaming of sharks normally indicates that the enemy is launching a severe attack. If you are bitten by a shark in your dream, your health, as well as your God-given purpose, assignments, and ministry, are under serious attack. Therefore, this requires urgent and immediate prayer inventions to disrupt the plans of the enemy. Like the Leviathan spirit, this demonic shark spirit also comes to drive fear within its victim. So be bold and use the Word of God to conquer it.

How to Pray

Be bold as a lion and stubborn as a mule against the kingdom of darkness. Refuse to give up or give in to the devil's schemes. Normally these demonic spirits are very stubborn, and so the individual must become more adamant than the enemy. Pray against every sickness and death attack. Cover your relationships, business, finances, health, and purpose under the blood of Jesus. Use the fire of God to destroy every demonic shark. Ask the Holy Spirit to hide you under the covers of his wings. Cry out to God for help and use your different spiritual weapons (please see my book entitled *Strategic Prayers: How To Wage Wars and Win* at www.sylvesterrankine.ca).

CHAPTER 11:
FINAL UNLOCKING (A-Z)

What is the one thing that all 7.9 billion people in the world have in common? The one thing we all experience? A dream. Yes, even though some people may not remember later what they dream, we all experience a dream in our lifetime. Spiritual warfare specialists teach us that when we have a dream and forget its details, sometimes a dream snatcher is at work. Here, a dream snatcher refers to demonic forces that are assigned to manipulate or erase memory so that the individual will have difficulty remembering the revelations or insights being given. In this regard, a spiritual attack needs a spiritual weapon. If you are being bombarded by forgetting your dreams, you must employ the weapons of prayer and fasting. Ask the Holy Spirit to cover the areas of your brain that are assigned to memory. Let's now do some final unlocking.

ALTAR

Unlocking the Dream: What Does an Altar Represent?

The altar normally represents *a place of sacrifice, slaughter, and death* (Genesis 8:20; Revelation 8:3). To unlock dreams with altars, please pay attention to the type of altar, who is at the altar, and the type of sacrifice that is being offered.

BLOOD

Unlocking the Dream: What Does Blood Represent?

Blood usually symbolizes *the life of the flesh, covenant, sacrifice, and atonement* (Leviticus 17:11–14; Isaiah 34:3; Romans 3:25).

BREAD

Unlocking the Dream: What Does Bread Represent?

Ever dream of seeing bread? Bread normally symbolizes *the staff of life, the Word of God, and provision* (John 6:35–58; John 6:5–9; Psalm 104:15; Matthew 6:11). To unlock dreams with bread, the dreamer must note the size or quantity of the bread. For example, is it a whole loaf of bread or a quarter of bread? Dreams of bread may indicate the level where the person's Bible-reading life is. If you

Chapter 11: Final Unlocking (A-Z)

see a whole bread, your Scripture reading is excellent. Oppositely, if you see a small piece of bread, you may need to spend more time in the Word of God.

BUS

Unlocking the Dream: What Does the Bus Represent?

The bus normally symbolizes *travel or movement into; relocation, destiny, and ministry.*

To unlock your dream, you must take note of the size of the bus. A big bus symbolizes a big assignment or purpose. Also, pay attention to whether you are on the bus versus outside. Another clue is to examine the people and the activities that are being done on the bus. Did you miss embarking on the bus? Constantly missing your bus is an indication of your purpose or assignments being attacked by the enemy or missed opportunities.

CANDLE/CANDLESTICK

Unlocking the Dream: What Does the Candle Represent?

The candle normally represents *light, the spirit of man and God, the Word of God, Christ, and the church* (Proverbs 20:27; Revelation 1:12–20; Psalm 119:105).

CHASED

Unlocking the Dream:
What Does Being Chased Represent?

This normally is not a good dream, and the key to dissecting this dream rests on emotions. How did you feel while being chased? Also, who was chasing you is another clue to unlocking its mystery.

DIRT DIGGING/DIGGING A HOLE

Unlocking the Dream:
What Does Digging a Hole Represent?

Once again, this dream must be interpreted within context. Notwithstanding, it normally symbolizes *death and funeral*.

DOOR

Unlocking the Dream:
What Does a Door Represent?

A door usually indicates *a way, entrance, portal, avenue, or opportunity* (2 Corinthians 2:12). Dreams with doors must be carefully examined. The dreamer must pay keen attention to the setting, as well as if the door is open or closed. Closed doors usually represent disappointments, hindrances, or blockages (Matthew 25:10; Revelation 3:7–8). If in the dream you shut the door to prevent an impending danger like an animal or thief from entering, this is a positive sign that the enemy does not have access. However, if the door was open and the enemy managed to enter, this is not good as it signifies that the enemy has access. This can be dangerous; therefore, the dreamers must examine their lives to see where the available opening is and permanently shut out the enemy.

EARTHQUAKE

Unlocking the Dream: What Do Earthquakes Represent?

An earthquake often means *judgment or the shaking of God* (Jeremiah 4:24; Revelation 16:18–19). Dreams of an earthquake are indicative of some impending danger. To unlock the dream, pay attention to the size of the earthquake, its location, time, and who is being affected.

FRUITS

Unlocking the Dream: What Does Fruit Represent?

Generally, fruit symbolizes *increase or multiplication, blessing, favor, and prosperity* (Psalm 21:10, Exodus 21:22; Ephesians 5:9; Philippians 1:11).

FRUIT PICKING

Unlocking the Dream

Pay keen attention to the size, fitness, color, and quantity of fruit. This is normally a good dream and represents "prosperity, favor, blessing, and breakthrough."

FRUIT EATING

Unlocking the Dream

Please note that eating in your sleep can be linked to witches trying to destroy your health and destiny as well as to bring you into demonic covenants. Please pay attention to the type of fruit as well as the condition of the fruit (rotten, young, green, ripe, etc.). So please interpret your dreams within context while using the tips given earlier as well as with the guidance of the Holy Spirit. Warfare experts will tell you to pray against evil night caterers and morning servers.

GATE

Unlocking the Dream: What Does a Gate Represent?

A gate often means *divine access, power, authority, and entrance* (Hebrews 13:12; Psalm 24:7). To unlock dreams with gates, the dreamer must examine the type, size, setting as well as whether the gate was closed or open. Key to note as well is who was standing at the gate or coming through the gate.

Chapter 11: Final Unlocking (A-Z)

HOUSE

Unlocking the Dream: What Does a House Represent?

A house often represents a *dwelling place, church, tabernacle, shelter, or residence* (John 14:2; Hebrews 3:1–6). To unlock dreams with a house, the dreamer must examine where the house was located as well as the condition of the house. A shaky house is indicative of a weak place as opposed to a strong structure, which may indicate security and strength. Also important is what activity was being carried out in the house.

IRON

Unlocking the Dream: What Does Iron Represent?

Iron often indicates *strength, power, stubbornness, and stronghold.*

JACKALS

Unlocking the Dream: What Do Jackals Represent?

Jackals usually indicate *evil, occult powers in operation, or scavengers of darkness.* The dreamer must look at what the jackal was doing, as well as how the presence of the jackals made them feel. If the jackals bite the dreamer, it is indicative of a satanic incision, an identification mark that delivers the dreamer to further demonic attacks. Therefore, urgent prayers must take place to neutralize its diabolic effect.

JEWELS

Unlocking the Dream: What Do Jewels Represent?

Jewels frequently mean "special treasures, prosperity, as well as God's people" (Malachi 3:17; Psalm 135:4). To unlock dreams with jewels, the dream interpreter must take note of the type of jewelry (gold, diamond, pearl, rubies, etc.). Also important is the color of the jewels as well as the size of the jewels.

KEYS

Unlocking the Dream: What Does a Key Represent?

A key normally represents *access, entry, authority, power, control over, to bind/loose, accountability, and prosperity* (Revelation 1:18; Revelation 9:1–2; Isaiah 22:22; Matthew 16:19).

Dream Encounter

A lady reported that she had a dream of a familiar dead person giving her a key. In the dream, her spirit man was alert as she was saying to herself, "But this person is dead; why should I take this key?" She started to rebuke the person and immediately found herself struggling to wake up as the person started to attack her.

Unlocking the Dream

This dream once again supports the fact that dreams must be interpreted within context as dreams can have double or multiple meanings. Even though the key generally represents access, notably for this dream, it wasn't good access. Clearly, the enemy was deceptive, and so accepting the key would be receiving death from the enemy. The devil used a familiar face to get the lady off guard and then proceeded to retaliate when the lady figured out his plans. May your spiritual eyes and spirit man be ever so sharp and alert. If you have a similar dream like this, you must bind and destroy every familiar spirit. Rebuke every devil associated with death while canceling and severing every graveyard spirit assignment.

LAND

Unlocking the Dream: What Does Land Represent?

Land typically represents *man's dwelling and earth* (Genesis 1:9). To unlock the dream, the interpreter must examine the size, condition, or quality of the land as well as the location. A barren land, land filled with garbage or stagnant water, usually indicates some impending danger or disaster. However, an excellent-looking land with wonderful vegetation may indicate prosperity.

MONEY

Unlocking the Dream: What Does Money Represent?

Money generally represents *power, authority, wealth, prosperity, and provision.* To unlock the dream, the interpreter must pay attention to who the money is being given to or received from. If the dreamer is giving away their money, in the good sense, it may indicate that the person has been elevated to the status of wealth distributor. Nevertheless, in the bad sense, it represents some evil powers or waster spirit that wants to deplete the individual's resources. Often, persons receive dreams of giving away money only to realize that their breakthroughs are suddenly blocked or their businesses or industry collapse. Satan and his minions are very deceptive, so dreams with money must be interpreted within context. Another point to note is that giving away money may also indicate coming into covenant with the person receiving the money. Good covenant brings blessings; oppositely, bad covenants breed curses or destruction.

NAKEDNESS

Unlocking the Dream: What Does Nakedness Represent?

Nakedness in a dream usually represents *some form of being stripped or exposed, humiliation, poverty, and shame* (Job 22:6; Habakkuk 3:9). Dreams of this kind must not be taken lightly because the enemy is always up to destroying people's lives.

OIL

Unlocking the Dream: What Does Oil Represent?

Oil normally symbolizes *the anointing as well as the Holy Spirit* (Isaiah 61:1; Luke 4:17; Acts 19:38).

ORGIES

Unlocking the Dream: What Do Orgies Represent?

Dreams of orgies normally indicate "enticement, initiation, evil covenant, and idolatry." If the dreamer was performing the act, the dream is geared towards initiation, pollution, or contamination, an ungodly covenant that breeds disaster and destruction of relationships, health, wealth, etc. If the dreamer was viewing the act being performed, it normally represents enticement and initiation.

PIT/PRISON

Unlocking the Dream: What Does Pit/Prison Represent?

Dreams of pit and prison usually signify *bondage,*

slavery, and being caged (Jeremiah 18:20; 1 Peter 3:19; Revelation 20:7).

QUIVER

Unlocking the Dream: What Does a Quiver Represent?

A quiver usually represents *covering and protection* (Psalm 127:5).

ROCK

Unlocking the Dream: What Does a Rock Represent?

A rock represents *strength, permanence, endurance, integrity, and shelter* (Job 24:8; Psalm 31:3, 95:1; Isaiah 2:10; Matthew 7:24–25).

Dream Encounter

Someone reported dreaming of a wicked person holding and throwing bigger rocks at them than the ones they were throwing at him.

Unlocking the Dream

Dreams of this nature suggest that the individual needs to get deeper into God. Spend greater time in the Word of God and prayer. It implies the enemy is exercising greater strength and advantages; therefore, the individual must spend more time in prayer to increase spiritual strength, insights, and revelations on how to conquer the enemy.

ROD

Unlocking the Dream: What Does a Rod Represent?

A rod often represents *guidance, rule, correction, and fruitfulness* (Psalm 23:4; Proverbs 13:24; Numbers 17).

ROOF

Unlocking the Dream: What Does a Roof Represent?

A roof generally represents *covering and oversight* (Matthew 8:8; Genesis 19:8; Luke 7:6).

ROOF (LEAKING/DAMAGED)

Unlocking the Dream: What Does a Damaged Roof Represent?

Dreams of a leaking roof or damaged roof indicate the person's coverage needs urgent attention. The individual is open to the attacks of the enemy. Therefore, a quick examination of one's life must be done to locate where the open access to the enemy is, and urgent corrective actions must be taken through strong prayer and fasting.

STORMS

Unlocking the Dream: What Does a Storm Represent?

Storms generally indicate *distress, danger, chaos, challenges, or trouble* (Psalm 55:8; Matthew 8:23–27; Luke 8:23). It is indicative of something God is about to do or Satan is plotting to enforce.

TRUMPET

Unlocking the Dream: What Does a Trumpet Represent?

Trumpet dreams generally represent *gathering, judgment, victory, blessings, the coming of Christ, and warfare* (Joshua 6:5; Hebrews 12:19).

UGLINESS

Unlocking the Dream: What Does Ugliness Represent?

Ugliness is generally indicative of demonic or evil spirits. The dreamer must be wise as a serpent because many times, the enemy appears as an angel of light, looking beautiful. A dreamer reported dreaming of seeing a deceased loved one looking beautiful and smiling. Upon the rebuking of this loved one, the sweet, beautiful image transformed into a vicious, ugly face and became violent. That's typically the nature of the devil and his allies, so be careful and exercise discernment when interpreting your dream.

VEHICLE

Unlocking the Dream: What Does a Vehicle Represent?

A vehicle typically represents *transportation or travel, purpose, fellowship, and ministry.* To unlock the dream, the interpreter must pay attention to the type of vehicle, its condition (speed, size, dirty or clean, old or new), its passenger, and what the vehicle is carrying. Also important is whether the vehicle has stopped, is moving, and the direction the vehicle is traveling in. Still, if the individual missed the vehicle or managed to go on the vehicle, a missed vehicle is normally indicative of disappointment or missed assignment or opportunity. The opposite is true if you caught the vehicle, and the vehicle is traveling. That normally speaks of mobility and hence is a positive dream.

VESSEL

Unlocking the Dream: What Does a Vessel Represent?

A vessel normally indicates the *human body, a container* (2 Timothy 2:21).

WOMB

Unlocking the Dream: What Does a Womb Represent?

A womb generally represents *conception, births, gestation, newness, or a new way of life*. Just as there is a physical womb, there is also such a thing as a spiritual womb. The spiritual womb is where innovations and cutting-edge concepts are birthed. Therefore, emotions, feelings, mindsets, or the seat of mental faculties are all connected to the womb. One pregnant dreamer reported dreaming of someone taking things from her womb. This is very dangerous as clearly, the enemy wanted to destroy her baby as he comes to kill, steal, and destroy. Dreams of this nature need urgent strategic prayers to cancel and sever every diabolical interruption of conception and birth.

WINDOW

Unlocking the Dream: What Do Windows Represent?

Windows usually represent *openness, blessings of heaven, inspirational thoughts, witty ideas, and intervention* (Genesis 6:16; Malachi 3:10). Windows are also indicative of a portal. The key to unlocking dreams with windows is to be keen on what is coming in through the window or whether the window was closed or opened. The dreamer must examine how they felt and examine the size as well as the setting of the window.

WORM

Unlocking the Dream: What Does a Worm Represent?

Worms generally represent an *instrument of judgment, that which is despised* (Matthew 9:44–48; Micah 7:17; Job 25:6; Psalm 22:16; Isaiah 14:14; Acts 12:23; Exodus 16:20).

X-RAY

Unlocking the Dream: What Does an X-ray Represent?

X-rays are pictures taken of the inside of something or someone. Dreams involving X-rays must not be taken lightly. Many people are attacked by practitioners of the Dark Arts who appear as doctors and nurses in dreams to administer X-rays, injections, medications, and surgeries. One dreamer reported being in a hospital and having an X-ray being administered on her body, and shortly after, organs were taken from her body. These dreams are serious, as witches and Dark Arts practitioners normally capture the image of people to later inflict pain, afflictions, sicknesses, and ultimate death on the dreamer. The dreamer must ask God to burn and destroy any image that was captured by the wicked one, as well as to destroy every diabolic X-ray equipment being used to attack.

YOUNG

Unlocking the Dream: What Does "Young" Represent?

Dreams involving "young…" normally signify *youthful exuberance, strength, overcoming, vitality, immaturity, or inexperience* (1 John 2:14; 1 Timothy 3:6). The key to unlocking the dream lies in what the "young" was doing as well as their temperament or nature.

ZIPPER

Unlocking the Dream: What Does a Zipper Represent?

A zipper typically suggests *privacy*. If the dreamer dreamt that their zipper was down, it basically symbolizes *exposure and disgrace*.

CHAPTER 12:
POWERFUL WARFARE PRAYERS

Prayer is one of the most effective spiritual disciplines and weapons that God has given to His people to help us unlock the hidden mysteries. Combined with fasting, prayer also has the propensity to wreak havoc in the enemy's kingdom. Whenever you receive a good dream, one that denotes blessings and favor, it is wise to pray and ask the Holy Spirit to let it manifest speedily. However, whenever you receive bad dreams, those that denote danger or attacks, you must take swift and speedy actions to cancel and sever the evil plots or plans of the adversary. Do not delay in destroying the devices of the enemy. Remember, early detection or interventions may save your life!

Our dreams, therefore, require that we pray strategically or employ the use of powerful warfare prayers when needed. In short, powerful warfare prayers require us to assess or interpret our dreams and use the various available spiritual weapons to effect and enforce God's plan over and against the powers of darkness. Powerful warfare prayers are those which are tailored using the Word of God. These prayers consist of legislating and taking authority in the name of Jesus. They involve praying strategically with the right mindset, position, and posture. We are not praying for victory; instead, we are praying from a position of victory because every knee must bow to Jesus—our King of all kings.

In order to master the art and skills of prayer, please see my book entitled *Strategic Prayers: How to Wage Wars and Win* (**www.sylvesterrankine.ca**). In the meantime, please make full use of the different examples of powerful warfare prayers concerning dreams, which are given below. You can be repetitive with the lines, words, and phrases as the Holy Spirit leads.

Chapter 12: Powerful Warfare Prayers

PRAYER: NUMBERS DREAMS

Any witchcraft powers projecting in my dream, I command you to die in the mighty name of Jesus!

Any number being used by my enemies against me, I command the curse attached to it to backfire now in the mighty name of Jesus.

Any diabolic curse that has been released by evil workers against me, I command you to break in Jesus' powerful name. Let the blessings of the Almighty God replace every curse now in Jesus' mighty name.

Let every curse the enemy has sent return both with power and assignment to my enemy now in Jesus' powerful name.

I stir up the number 8 of a new beginning to work for my life now!

I call forth the number of grace (5) and grace upon grace (25) to manifest great things in my life speedily.

I call forth the right connections to locate me now.

I activate the number (24) representing the

government to work for me now in Jesus' name.

Oh, Almighty God, anything the enemy is using as a point of contact with my name and number on it, let it catch on fire now in Jesus' great name.

I break every evil connection and cord connecting me to the moon and galaxies to destroy my life.

I decree and declare, Psalm 91, the sun shall not smite me by day nor the moon by night, but You shall preserve my soul even now and forever more.

Amen.

Chapter 12: Powerful Warfare Prayers

PRAYER: COLORS DREAMS

As God's end-time warrior, I rise to destroy every diabolical attack of the adversary.

I decree and declare that the blood of Jesus Christ of Nazareth now neutralizes and nullifies the effect of every evil black arrow of depression, oppression, and suppression.

I announce that the blood of Jesus now wipes out every red arrow of contention that has been released against my life and loved ones.

I decree and declare that I shall not die, but with long life, I shall live. I put a stop order to every dark spell and destroy every demonic force of the dark world.

I illuminate my room, homes, and office with the light of God and command the presence of the Almighty God to overtake my environment.

Let every evil strongman wearing black clothing be exposed and destroyed by the fire of the Almighty God.

I command weeping and destruction to be far from my household, far from my street, far from my family, far from my community, and my nation in Jesus' powerful name.

I superimpose the joy of the Lord to dispel and destroy every sadness and reinforce me daily in Jesus' miraculous name.

Chapter 12: Powerful Warfare Prayers

PRAYER: DEMONIC BIRDS DREAMS

I blind the eyes of every demonic bird.

Every monitoring spirit is to be disturbed in the mighty name of Jesus.

I interrupt every diabolic frequency assigned to spy on me.

Heavenly Father, release angels of like stature of Gabriel and Michael and destroy every demonic bird in high and low places.

I summon the angels of God to cage every demonic bird in the abyss.

O God, torment these demonic birds now and forever in Jesus' name.

PRAYERS: INSECTS/REPTILES DREAMS

Demonic Ants

God of Elijah, answer by fire and blind the eyes of every demonic ant in Jesus' name.

I rebuke every graveyard spirit and send you back to the enemy's camp in Jesus' name.

In the mighty name of Jesus, I command every witchcraft spell to be permanently broken from my life! Now!

I crush the head of every demonic ant and render your assignment powerless.

I activate Psalm 118:17 (KJV) and declare that "I shall not die but [I shall] live [with long life]."

You, spirit of pain and affliction, I bind you in the mighty name of Jesus and give you a new assignment, become the footstool of Jesus now.

Spirit of infirmity, loosen your hold from off my life in Jesus' name. I bind every demon of death and render your assignments null and void. I superimpose life over and

Chapter 12: Powerful Warfare Prayers

against death.

I enforce Isaiah 54:17 (KJV) "No weapon formed against [me] shall prosper." O God of Daniel, pursue my pursuer and destroy my destroyer in Jesus' name. As of today, I rewrite the script, life instead of death and joy instead of pain shall be my portion all the days of my life, amen, amen and amen.

Demonic Bats

I come against every hunter of the night in Jesus' name.

Every demonic vampire bat, you will not suck my blood to draw my virtue, fall down and die in Jesus' name.

Every witchcraft power backfires now in Jesus' mighty name.

I interrupt the soundwave of every diabolic bat; I command confusion to overtake you now.

I annihilate every eavesdropping spirit, and I decree and declare I shall not be monitored in Jesus' name.

Demonic Spiders

Oh God of Elijah, answer by fire, burn and

destroy every spiderweb now.

Oh God of Daniel, rescue me from every demonic entrapment.

I loosen myself from the snare of the spider and break free from every evil enticement.

I decree and declare that I shall not be tricked.

O God of Samson, arise, expose, and destroy every deceiver in my life in Jesus' mighty name.

I command the volcanic fire of God to destroy every demonic spider that comes to poison me in Jesus' name.

Demonic Lizards

Oh Lord, strike my destiny blockers with Your lightning and thunder now!

Oh my God, send Your angels to remove and destroy every hindrance in my life.

I command every ancestral spirit to receive the fire of the Almighty God now!

I break free from every ancestral curse in the mighty name of Jesus.

Every spirit of the lizard, die in Jesus' name.

Chapter 12: Powerful Warfare Prayers

Demonic Snakes

Oh, Heavenly Father, I repent of every sin.

I sever the head of every demonic serpentine spirit in Jesus' name.

With my feet, I crush the head of every serpent.

I loosen myself free from every perversion and seduction in Jesus' name.

Oh, Jehovah-Gibbor, destroy every demonic snake with Your fire now.

I declare that I will not be mesmerized, confused, or consumed.

Every marine kingdom spirit, what are you waiting for? Die in Jesus' name!

I cover my mind, body, soul, and spirit under the blood of Jesus Christ of Nazareth now and forever in Jesus' name.

Demonic Cockroaches

Father, I repent of any sin that gives the enemy the legal right to afflict me.

Lord Jesus, cleanse my life of all evil pollution with Your blood.

Any evil cockroach assigned against me,

die in the mighty name of Jesus.

Any witchcraft power assigned against my progress be destroyed in the mighty name of Jesus.

Oh Lord, mash up every evil coven and torment my tormentors in Jesus' name.

Chapter 12: Powerful Warfare Prayers

PRAYER: DEMONIC ANIMALS DREAMS

I bind and cast out any demonic animals that are working against me in Jesus' name.

I bind and rebuke every demonic animal that is operating in the high and low places in Jesus' name.

I command the sword of God to cut off the feet of every demonic animal that are swift to cause trouble.

My life shall not be hindered by any demonic animals in the mighty name of Jesus.

Lord, send Your angels to smite every demonic tiger, dog, and cow.

Oh Lord, teach my hands to war and my fingers to fight against every demonic animal that comes to destroy my finance through sickness.

Oh God, like David, teach my hands to destroy every demonic bear.

Oh God, like Samson, teach my hands to destroy every demonic donkey in Jesus' name.

PRAYERS: ELEMENTS OF THE WATER DREAM

Leviathan Spirit

Every evil spirit operating from the waters against me, fall down and die.

Oh Lord, put a hook in Leviathan's nostril now in Jesus' name.

Destroy its arrogance and make a public spectacle of the Leviathan spirit in Jesus' name.

I activate Psalm 35 against every Leviathan spirit and command the angels of God to annihilate every proud water spirit in Jesus' name.

Jehovah-Gibbor, contend with them that contend with me.

Fight against those that fight against me. Take hold of the shield and buckler and stand up for my help.

I activate Psalm 74:14, Oh God, break the head of the Leviathan serpent in pieces with Your flaming sword and give it as food to inhabitants of the wilderness.

I cover my relationship under the blood

of Jesus. I command the sword of God to destroy every Leviathan-piercing tongue. I cripple and paralyze the Leviathan with the Word of God, and I command you to be tamed and destroyed forever by the power of the Holy Spirit.

Demonic Fish

My Heavenly Father burns out every demonic fish from my body in the powerful name of Jesus.

Lord Jesus, I ask that You purge my stomach, bloodstreams, organs, tissues, and cells with Your blood.

My Father, restore my virtue, passion, zeal, energy, and strength in the mighty name of Jesus.

Every night caterer and morning server feeding me in my sleep, scatter in the mighty name of Jesus.

I command my body to reject every demonic substance now in Jesus' name. Affliction, hear the Word of the Lord, scatter in Jesus' name!

Spirit of infirmity, I bind you! Loosen your hold from off my life in the name of Jesus. As of today, I seal every area of my life with the blood of Jesus and declare no demonic fish shall locate me in Jesus' mighty name.

DEMONIC SHARK

Oh God of Moses, hasten to part my sea and expose every demonic shark that is operating against my health, wealth, and purpose in Jesus' name.

I command the sledgehammer of the Almighty God to break every shark tooth quickly in Jesus' powerful name.

I activate the fire of God and blind the eyes of every demonic shark now in Jesus' name.

I command every demonic shark to be destroyed by the power of the Holy Ghost.

Oh, Jesus, my Savior, use Your blood and wipe out every demonic marking from off my body in Jesus' powerful name.

I speak health and healing over my body. I activate Jeremiah 17:14–15 (KJV), "Heal me, O Lord, and I shall be healed; save me, [O Lord,] and I shall be saved: for thou art my praise."

I cover my relationships, businesses, finances, and health under the blood of

Chapter 12: Powerful Warfare Prayers

Jesus. May every shark spirit die by the fire of God in the powerful name of Jesus Christ of Nazareth ((Repeat 7 times)).

Conclusion

In the year 2021, I received a series of shocking dreams that collided in February 2022. One dream concerned my community being invaded by soldiers and everyone being ordered to stay inside or else they would die! Another revealed a severe famine and the atrocities that come with it. Then in February 2022, I received a final dream with the same theme of devastation and danger. I dreamt of a bomber heading towards a high-rise building. I woke up in bewilderment with my mouth wide open and my emotions quite stirred up. I knew I had to pray immediately! To my amazement, when I turned on my television the next day, it was Russia and Ukraine at war. Wow! This was what the Lord had been revealing to me all this time, but for some reason, I was too busy caught up with the everyday affairs of life that I almost missed it.

In light of this, as we journey to the end of this book, I am compelled to ask the same questions that we began the trip with. Are you making the most of your dreams? Are you taking advantage of the opportunity each dream is pregnant with? After receiving all these revelations, better yet, can you afford not to take your dreams more seriously? Do you want to be ahead of the game or ahead of your competitors or rivals? Do you want to outsmart the enemy? Do you desire to have dominion in every sphere of your life? If your answer to any of these questions is yes, then the need arises for you to start unlocking your dreams.

Unlocking the Dream

You must employ the use of the various dream tips given in this book to assist with unlocking the hidden treasures that await you. Pay keen attention to detail, color, number, frequency, time, etc. Record your dreams at once after waking. Pray and ask the Holy Spirit to cover your dream life and to remind you of the details of your dream. Lean on the Holy Spirit like Joseph, Solomon, and Daniel to access great wisdom and insights into your dream unlocking. The Holy Spirit is the greatest teacher and the originator of all wisdom. When faced with a puzzling or difficult dream, don't become anxious and flustered. Instead, be patient, pray, listen, and expect God to reveal Himself.

Notwithstanding, skillful dream interpretation may not come overnight, but at least if we try or start to interpret one dream at a time, we will eventually become skillful at unlocking the next upcoming dream. It is such a waste when we receive dreams that are given for advancement, and we allow them to slip by or be aborted by the enemy. Now more than ever, God is downloading dreams to His people with the intention to bless and guide them. The opposite is also true; now more than ever, the devil is also launching his vicious attacks against people and their God-given destinies through dreams. Can we afford not to start unlocking our dreams?

Unlocking our dreams and those of our loved ones is worth even more than any treasures, gold, diamonds, or billion-dollar ideas. What am I talking about? Life! Unlocking the dream could save your life and those

Conclusion

of your loved ones. When you interpret your dreams correctly, at the right time and season, you are able to nullify the threats of the enemy. I believe this is priceless!

Yes, you can save the lives of your loved ones. You can save the destinies of your children. You can preserve and protect the citizens of your community, nations, and countries. Agree with God's kingdom assignments for your life today. Do not let the enemy delay, disrupt, or deny your blessings or breakthroughs. God has given us a powerful tool by which to conquer. It's called *Unlocking the Dream*. Become a dream interpreter today. Take control. Take dominion of your life. It's time to start unlocking the dream!

APPENDIX

NUMBER SYMBOLISM

Number 9	Meanings	Additional Information
Christian	Nine (9) symbolizes *the number of the Holy Spirit, divine completeness or finality, and fruit of the Spirit*.	Galatians 5:22–23; 1 Corinthians 12:8–10
Jewish/ Hebrew	The Hebrew words *Teshah* and *Tishah* are used for nine and symbolize *finality, judgment, harvest, fruitfulness, womb, duality (good/evil), concealment, truth, lovingkindness, gaze, the fruit of the Spirit, and hour of prayer.* The corresponding pictographic meaning for nine is *basket, good/evil, snake, surround, knot, twist, spiral, fruitfulness, repentance, and judgment.*	

Dark Arts practitioners	Nine (9) is also linked to the goddess energy in many traditions. The Tarot card "The 9 of Cups" is considered to be the wish card. Thus, many of these practitioners use the Tarot card 9 as a symbol of the completion of a process.	
Number 10	**Meanings**	**Additional Information**
Christian	Ten represents *law and responsibility, testimony, completeness, order, and a complete and perfect number, as are 3, 7, and 12.*	Genesis 24; Genesis 31:7; Genesis 45:23

Jewish/ Hebrew	The Hebrew words *Eser* and *Asarah* are used for the number 10 and mean *completed cycle, divine order, measure, group (congregation, body or kingdom good/evil), blessings or judgment; tithe (a tenth part represents the whole).* The corresponding pictographic meaning for ten is *hand, worship, work, deed, fist, power, and congregation.*	God sent ten plagues on ancient Egypt, representing His complete judgment. The Ten Commandments (Exodus 20)

Number 11	Meanings	Additional Information
Christian	Number 11 represents *disorder, chaos, lawlessness, incompleteness, disintegration, and judgment.*	Genesis 11; Genesis 36:40–43; Judges 16:6, 3:3

Jewish/ Hebrew	The Hebrew words *achat esre* and *achad esar* are used for the number 11 and mean *outsider, disorder, disorganization, incomplete, lack (12 - 1), excess (10 + 1);* both signify *imperfection, transition moving back to 10 or ahead to 12, betrayal, idolatry, bribery, and rebellion to the heavenly authority.* *Good sense*: eleven represents *the prophetic realm.* *Bad sense*: eleven represents *counterfeit and divination.* The corresponding pictographic meaning is *open hand or container, to receive, possession, or ownership.*	Eleven can also depict a place of godly transition.

Number 12	Meanings	Additional Information
Christian	Numeral twelve represents *God's power and authority, perfect governmental foundation, completeness, and anointed service.*	Leviticus 24; Matthew 28:12; Luke 2:42; 1 Samuel 28:3–6; Numbers 27:21

Appendix

Jewish/ Hebrew	The Hebrew words *shtayim esre* and *shnayim asar* are used for the number 12 and mean *perfect government, organization, order, united, perfect subdivision of time (12 hours of the day; 12 months in the year; 12 disciples; 12 tribes; 12 constellations.* The corresponding pictographic meaning is *shepherd's hook/staff, teaching, learning, goading, protection, yoke, and bind.*	

Number 13	Meanings	Additional Information
Christian	13 represents *rebellion, backsliding, and lawlessness.*	In the Book of Revelation, "the dragon," a symbol of Satan representing rebellion, is said to occur 13 times.
Jewish/ Hebrew	The Hebrew word *shlosh esre* translates to the number 13 and symbolizes *love, covenant, unity, and eternity.* The corresponding pictographic meaning is *water, chaos, immersion, womb, and blood.*	Thirteen (13) is the age at which a Jewish male becomes obligated to follow Jewish law; hence it is associated with a new beginning.

| Dark Arts practitioners | For occult practitioners, the Tarot card number 13 represents death. Many Dark Arts practitioners use the number 13 as a remarkable force for transition to another level. They embrace the notion that on the 13th day after fertilization, the embryo forms the umbilical cord and is attached to the mother; thus, special energy is said to be gained on the 13th day. Still, witches are said to gather in covens of thirteen; thus, the occult embraced the number thirteen and used various symbolism relating to this number. For example, lighting 13 candles. | On Friday, October 13, 1307, King Philip IV of France ordered a mass arrest of Templars, which later resulted in severe torture and burning at the stake. Thus, Friday the 13th, synonym with the number thirteen, holds the stigma of "bad luck." Many buildings skip numbering the 13th floor, while many airlines skip numbering the thirteenth row. |

Appendix

Number 14	Meanings	Additional Information
Christian	Numeral 14 represents deliverance and salvation.	Matthew 1:17
Jewish/ Hebrew	The Hebrew words *arbah esre* and *arba'ah asar* are used for the number 14, meaning *a multiple of seven, double measure (7 + 7), the number of the Messiah, to reproduce, recreate, disciple, servant, and bondservant.* The corresponding pictographic meaning is *seed, life, fish, heir, productiveness, continuity, permanence, prophetic, and multiplication.*	On the 14th day of the first month (Nissan), God saved the firstborn of Israel as well as delivered the children of Israel out of bondage from Egypt hence the celebration of the Passover today.
Dark Arts practitioners	The 14th card in the Tarot is Temperance, which shows a picture of an angel who is considered to have a connection with the underworld.	

Number 15	Meanings	Additional Information
Christian	Numeral 15 represents *rest*.	2 Kings 20:1–6; 2 Kings 20; Isaiah 38:5; Hosea 3; Luke 3:1–3; Galatians 1:18
Jewish/ Hebrew	The Hebrew words *chamesh esre* and *chamish'a asar* translate to 15 and symbolize *a multiple of five, salvation, healing, redemption, prolonging, stepping up, ascending and fullness, and elevation from the physical to the spiritual.* The corresponding pictographic meaning is *thorn, to surround, support, protect, wheel, snake.*	

Appendix

Dark Arts practitioners	Practitioners of the Dark Arts use the 15th card in the Tarot to represent the devil.	
Number 16	**Meanings**	**Additional Information**
Christian	Numeral 16 represents *love and loving*.	2 Kings 15:2
Jewish/ Hebrew	The Hebrew words *shesh esre* and *shisha asar* represent the number 16 and mean *without boundaries or limits, a new beginning, covenant.* The corresponding pictographic meaning is *eye, well of water, vision literal or prophetic, perception.*	

Number 17	Meanings	
Christian	Numeral 17 represents *overcoming the enemy and complete victory.*	
Jewish/ Hebrew	The Hebrew words *shva esre* and *shiv'a asar* translate to 17 and symbolize *completeness, divine order, and congregation.* *Bad sense*: 17 represents *immaturity and naivety.* The corresponding pictographic meaning is *mouth, opening, speech, blow, and scatter. The mouth reveals whether one is mature or not.*	

Appendix

Number 18	Meanings	
Christian	Numeral 18 is symbolic of bondage.	
Jewish/ Hebrew	The Hebrew words *shmoneh esre* and *shmonah asar* are used for 18 and symbolize *life, prayer, temple worship, devotion, offering, charity, being loosed or freed, and sacrifice.* *Bad sense:* 18 represents *judgment, destruction, captivity, and bondage.* The corresponding pictographic meaning is *trail, journey, hunt, righteous, upright one, and justice.*	

Number 19	Meanings	
Christian	Numeral 19 is symbolic of God's perfect order with regards to His judgment.	
Jewish/ Hebrew	The Hebrew words *tsha esre* and *tish a'asar* translate to 19 and symbolize *divine order, judgment, and truth revealed or concealed.* The corresponding pictographic meaning is *sun on the horizon, time, imitation of God or enemy, and circle.*	

Number 20	Meanings	Additional Information
Christian	Numeral 20 represents *a complete or perfect waiting period.*	1 Samuel 5:7
Jewish/ Hebrew	The Hebrew word *esrim* translates numeral 20 and means *manhood, age of accountability for service, war and worship, expectation, divine order, maturity, manhood, accountability, and being counted.* The corresponding pictographic meaning is *authority, beginning, a man's head, first, top.*	

Appendix

Dark Arts practitioners	Dark Arts practitioners believe twenty has strong spiritual power and believe when seen, guardian angels are sending messages to individuals in dreams.	
Number 21	**Meanings**	
Christian	Numeral 21 represents the great wickedness of rebellion and sin.	
Jewish/ Hebrew	The Hebrew words *esrim v'achat* and *esrim v'echad* translate to the number 21 and mean a tripling of 7 (7 x 3 = 21) multiplication of rest, holiness. *Bad sense*: 21 represents *judgment, anti-Messiah.* The corresponding pictographic meaning is *teeth, to devour, chew on, destroy, think about, ponder, fire, tongues of fire, sharpen, eat or consume.*	

Number 22	Meanings	
Christian	Numeral 22 represents *a concentration of disorganization*.	
Jewish/Hebrew	The Hebrew words *esrim v' shtayim* and *esrim v' shnayim* translate to numeral 22 and mean *the whole of the Word of God, the beginning and the end, the Alpha and Omega.* *Bad sense:* 22 is the doubling of 11 and represents *complete wickedness, anti-Christ, doing what is right in the sight of own eyes.* The corresponding pictographic meaning is the seal of God or the mark of the enemy, completion signal, monument, government, and authority, whether wicked or evil.	

Appendix

Number 24	Meanings	Additional Information
Christian	Numeral 24 indicates priesthood and the worship of God.	1 Chronicles 24
Jewish/ Hebrew	The Hebrew words *esrim v'arba* and *esrim v'arba'a* translate to 24 and represent *heavenly government and worship, dividing time, priesthood, watchmen, all parts working together in the service of YHWH.* Bad sense: 24 represents *those that oppose the government, authority, or worship of God.*	

Number 25	Meanings	Additional Information
Christian	Numeral 25 represents *grace upon grace.*	2 Kings 15:23; 2 Kings 18:2; John 1:14
Jewish/ Hebrew	The Hebrew word *esriym* translates to 25. Twenty means redemption, and five means grace; thus, twenty-five symbolizes grace upon grace, the forgiveness of sin.	

Unlocking the Dream

Number 40	Meanings	Additional Information
Christian	Numeral 40 represents *a period of great testing, trial, and probation.*	Jesus fasted for 40 days and 40 nights and afterward was tempted by the devil. The earth was judged by flood rains during the time of Noah, which lasted for 40 days. The Israelites wandered in the wilderness for 40 years. Jonah warned Nineveh for forty days. (Genesis 7:1–12; Josh. 5:6; Ezekiel 4:6; Exodus 24:18; Deuteronomy 29:3–4; Jonah 3:1–10; Mark 1:13)
Jewish/ Hebrew	40 represents *transition or change, the concept of renewal or new beginning, spiritual renewal,* and *personal growth/renewal.*	

Appendix

Numbers	Meanings	Additional info.
50	Numeral 50 represents liberty, freedom, Pentecost, deliverance, or freedom from a burden, jubilee.	Genesis 8, Leviticus 25:10–11; Isaiah 3:3; Esther 5:14; Acts 2:1–4
100	Symbolizes fullness, full measure, and full recompense.	
600	Symbolizes warfare.	
1000	Symbolizes maturity, mature service, divine completeness, and glory of God.	

Bibliography

Alper, Cuneyt M., Luntz, Michal, Takahashi, Haruo, Ghadiali, Samir N., Swarts, J. Douglas, Teixeira, Miriam S., Csa' ka' Nyi, Zsuzsanna, Yehudai, Noam, Kania, Romain and Poe, Dennis S. "Panel 2: Anatomy Eustachin Tube, Middle ear, mastoid-Anatomy, Physiology, pathophysiology, and Pathogenesis." *American Academy Otolaryngology-Head and Neck Surgery* 156 (4S), S22–S40 (2017). Accessed February 3, 2022. http://doi.10.1177/0194599816647959

Alshami, Abeer A., Alharthi, Shatha, Binshabaib, Munerah, and Wahi, Monika. "Tooth Morphology Overview. Human Teeth." *IntechOpen* (2019). Accessed February 4, 2022. http://doi.10.5772/intechopen.87153

Baker, Phil, Furlong, Mick, Southern, Suzanne, and Harris, Stephen. "The Potential Impact of Red Fox Vulpes Vulpes Predation in Agricultural Landscapes in Lowland Britain." *Wildlife Biology*, 12 (1), 39–50 (2006). Accessed February 8, 2022. https://doi.org/10.2981/0909-6396(2006)12[39:TPIORF]2.0.CO;2

Brito, Luiz F., Miglior, Filippo, Oliveira, Hinayah R., Houlahan, Kerry, Fonseca, Pablo A.S., Lam, Stephanie, Butty, Adrien M., Seymour, Dave J., Vargus, Giovana, Chud, Tatiane C.S., Silva, Fabyano F., Baes, Christine F., Canovas, Angela, Miglior, Filippo, and Schenkel, Flavio S. "Genetic Mechanisms Underlying Feed Utilization and Implementation of Genomic Selection for Improved Feed Efficiency in Dairy Cattle." *Canadian Journal of Animal Science*, 100 (4), 587–604 (2020). Accessed February 8, 2022. https://doi.org/10.1139/cjas-2019-0193

Burgas, Daniel, Ovaskainen, Otso, Blanchet, F. Guillaume, and Byholm, Patrik. "The Ghost of the Hawk: Top Predator Shaping Bird Communities in Space and Time." *Frontiers in Ecology and Evolution* (2021). 9:638039 https://doi.org/10.3389/fevo.2021.638039

Centers for Disease Control and Prevention [CDC]. "Diseases Directly Transmitted by Rodents" (2017). Accessed February 5, 2022. https://www.cdc.gov/rodents/diseases/direct.html

Cismaru, Gabriel, Muresan, Lucian, Mihai, Puiu, Rosu, Radu, Gusetu, Gabriel, Cismaru, Andrei, Pop, Dana, and Zdrenghea, Dumitru. "Cardiac Anatomy for the Electrophysiologist with Emphasis on the Left Atrium and Pulmonary Veins. Human Anatomy." *IntechOpen* (2017). http://doi.10.5772/intechopen.69120

Clancy, Cara L., Kubasiewicz, Laura M., Raw, Zoe, and Cooke, Fiona. "Science and Knowledge of Free-Roaming Donkeys: A Critical Review." *The Journal of Wildlife Management* (2021). Accessed February 9, 2022. https://doi.org/10.1002/jwmg.22090

Creel, Scott, Christianson, David, and Schuette, Paul. "Glucocorticoid Stress Responses of Lions in Relationship to Group Composition, Human Land Use, and Proximity to People." *Conservation Physiology 1* (1) (2013). Accessed February 7, 2022. https://doi.org/10.1093/conphys/cot021

Durkin, Emily S., Cassidy, Steven T., Gilbert, Rachel, Richardson, Elise A., Roth, Allison M., Shablin, Samanta, and Keiser, Carl N. "Parasites of Spiders: Their Impacts on Host Behavior and Ecology." *The Journal of Arachnology*, *49* (3), 281–298 (2021). https://doi.org/10.1636/JoA-S-20-087

Edut, Shahaf and Eilam, David. "Rodents in Open Space Adjust Their Behavioral Response to the Different Risk Levels During Barn-Owl Attack." *BMC Ecology 3* (10) (2003). Accessed February 7, 2022. https://doi.org/10.1186/1472-6785-3-10

Erdogan, Bilgen. *Anatomy and Physiology of the Hair* (2017). Accessed February 3, 2022. http://dx.doi.org/10.5772/67269

Graphics/Images accessed April 6, 2022. https://pixabay.com

Hashimoto, Yukihiko and Anrui, Tomohito. "Establishment of Management Plan by Sighting Reports of Asiatic Black Bears (Ursus Thibetanus): A Case Study in Oze National Park, Central Japan. In (Ed.), National Parks-Management and Conservation."

Bibliography

IntechOpen (2017). https://doi.org/10.5772/intechopen.73313

Hesford, Nicholas, Baines, David, Smith, A. Adam, and Ewald, Julie A. "Distribution of Mountain Hares Lepus Timidus in Scotland in 2016/2017 and Changes Relative to Earlier Surveys in 1995/1996 and 2006/2007." *Wildlife Biology*, 2020 (2). https://doi.org/10.2981/wlb.00650

Hobbs, Rebecca J., and Hinds, Lyn A. "Could Current Fertility Control Methods Be Effective for Landscape-Scale Management of Populations of Wild Horses (Equus Caballus) in Australia." *Wildlife Research, 45* (3), 195–207 (2018). Accessed February 8, 2022. https://doi.org/10.1071/WR17136

Hoffman, Matthew. "Picture of the Brain" (2021). Accessed February 3, 2022. https://www.webmd.com/brain/picture-of-the-brain

Hongo, Hitomi, Ishiguro, Naotaka, Watanobe, Takuma, Shigehara, Nobuo, Anezaki, Tomoko, The Long, Vu, Binh, Dang Vu, Tien, Nguyen Trong, and Nam, Nguyen Huu. "Variation in Mitochondrial DNA of Vietnamese Pigs: Relationships with Asian Domestic Pigs and Ryukyu Wild Boars." *Zoological Science, 19* (11), 1329–1335 (2002). Accessed February 8, 2022. https://doi.org/10.2108/zsj.19.1329

Israili, Zafar H. "Effect of Pigeon Keeping on Health and Family Life." *Journal of Community Public Health Nursing, 3*:190 (2017). https://doi:10.4172/2471-9846.1000190

Jones, Peter E., Svendsen, Jon C., Borger, Luca, Champneys, Toby, Consuegra, Sofia, Jones, Joshua A. H., and Garcia de Leaniz, Carlos. "One Size Does Not Fit All: Inter-And Intraspecific Variation in the Swimming Performance of Contrasting Freshwater Fish." *Conservation Physiology 8* (1) (2020). Accessed February 7, 2022. https://doi.org/10.1093/conphys/coaa126

Kroesen, Laura P., Hik, David S., and Cherry, Seth G. "Patterns of Decadal, Seasonal and Daily Visitation to Mineral Licks, A Critical Resource Hotspot for Mountain Goats Oreamnos Americanus in the Rocky Mountains." *Wildlife Biology*, 2020 (4), 00736. https://

doi.org/10.2981/wlb.00736

Landry, Jean-Marc, Borelli, Jean-Luc, and Drouilly, Marine. "Interactions between Livestock Guarding Dogs and Wolves in Southern French Alps." *Journal of Vertebrate Biology*, *69* (3), 20078.1–18 (2020). Accessed February 8, 2022. https://doi.org/10.25225/jvb.20078

Lanzendorfer, Joy. "10 Ravishing Facts about Raven" (2021). Accessed February 10, 2022. https://www.mentalfloss.com/article/53295/10-fascinating-facts-about-ravens

Li, LePing and Kazemi, Mojtaba. "Fluid Pressurization in Cartilages and Menisci in the Normal and Repaired Human Knees. Modeling and Simulation in Engineering." *IntechOpen*, Prof. Catalin Alexandru (Ed.), ISBN: 978-953-51-0012-6, 2012, http://www.intechopen.com/books/modeling-and-simulation-inengineering/fluid-pressurization-in-cartilages-and-menisci-in-the-normal-and-repaired-human-knees

Marsh, Laura K. "A Taxonomic Revision of the Saki Monkeys, Pithecia Desmarest, 1804." *Neotropical Primates, 21* (1), 1–165 (2014). Accessed February 8, 2022. https://doi.org/10.1896/044.021.0101

Mete, Asli and Akbudak, Ilknur H. "Functional Anatomy and Physiology of Airway. Tracheal Intubation." *IntechOpen* (2018). Accessed February 4, 2022. http://doi.10.5772/intechopen.77037

Mondol, Samrat, Navya, R., Athreya, Vidya, Sunagar, Kartik, Selvaraj, Velu Mani, and Uma, Ramakrishnan. "A Panel of Microsatellites to Individually Identify Leopards and Its Application to Leopard Monitoring in Human Dominated Landscapes." *National Library of Medicine. BMC Genet, 10 (79)* (2009). Accessed February 28, 2022. http://doi.10.1186/1471-2156-10-79

Ortiz, Ernesto and Possani, Lourival D. (2015). "The Unfulfilled Promises of Scorpion Insectotoxins." *Journal of Venomous Animals and Toxins Including Tropical Diseases. 21* (16). Accessed February 6, 2022. https://rdcu.be/cGucZ https://doi.org/10.1186/s40409-015-0019-6

Bibliography

Pahari, Sushanta, Bickford, David, Fry, Brayan G., and Kini, Manjunatha. "Expression Pattern of Three-Finger Toxin and Phospholipase A2 Genes in the Venom Glands of Two Sea Snakes, Lapemis Curtus and Acalyptophis Peronei: Comparison of Evolution of These Toxins in Land Snakes, Sea Kraits and Sea Snakes." *BMC Evolutionary Biology 7* (175) (2007). Accessed February 7, 2022. https://doi.org/10.1186/1471-2148-7-175

Pas, An and Dubey, J. P. "Fatal Toxoplasmosis in Sand Cat Felis Margarita." *Journal of Zoo and Wildlife Medicine, 39* (3), 362–369 (2008). Accessed February 8, 2022. https://doi.org/10.1638/2007-0149.1

Prendergast, Peter M. "Anatomy of the Face and Neck." *Venus Medical Cosmetic Surgery* (2012). Accessed February 4, 2022. http://doi.10.1007/978-3-642-21837-8_2

Rankine, Sylvester. *Kill That Dog: Deliverance from the Dog Spirit.* Diamond Destiny Publishing: Jamaica, 2018.

Reyes, Luis Fernando Basanta, Carrasco, Manual Calderon, and Martin, Angel Rodriguez. "The Limit to the Density of Species (A Reflection on Human Intervention in Conservation and Its Effects). In (Ed.), Birds-Challenges and Opportunities for Business, Conservation and Research." *IntechOpen* (2020). https://doi.org/10.5772/intechopen.97436

Salazar, Juan J., Ramirez, Ana I., Hoz, Rosa De, Salobrar-Garcia, Elena, Rojas, Pilar, Fernandez-Albarral, Jose A., Lopez-Cuenca, Ines, Rojas, Blanca, Trivino, Alberto, and Ramirez, Jose M. "Anatomy of the Human Optic Nerve: Structure and Function". *IntechOpen* (2018). Accessed February 3, 2022. http://doi.10.5772/intechopen.79827

Sarvi, Masoud Nasiri. "Hip Fracture: Anatomy, Causes, and Consequences. Total Hip Replacement." *IntechOpen* (2018). Accessed February 4, 2022. http://doi.10.5772/intechopen.75946

Seltmann, Anne, Czirjak, Gabor A., Courtiol, Alexandre, Bernard, Henry, Struebig, Matthew J., and Voight, Christian C. "Habitat Disturbances Results in Chronic Stress and Impaired Health Status in Forest-Dwelling Paleotropical Bats." *Conservation Physiology* 5 (1) (2017). Accessed February 7, 2022. https://doi.org/10.1093/conphys/cox020

Serrezuela, Ruthber Rodriguez, Zamora, Roberto Sagaro, and Reyes, Enrique Maranon. "Control Strategy for Underactuated Multi-Fingered Robot Hand Movement Using Electromyography Signal with Wearable Myo Armband. Biosensors" *IntechOpen* (2020). Accessed February 4, 2022. http://doi.10.5772/intechopen.93767

Sikka, Pilleriin, Revonsuo, Antti, Sandman, Nils, Tuominen, Jarno, and Valli, Katja. "Dreams Emotions: A Comparison of Home Dream Reports with Laboratory Early and Late REM Dream Reports." *Journal of Sleep Res. 27*, 206–214 (2018). http://doi.1111/jsr.12555

Singh, Rajani. "Cerebellum: Its Anatomy Functions and Diseases." *IntechOpen* (2020). Accessed February 3, 2022. http://doi.10.5772/intechopen.93064

Strong, James. *The New Strong's Expanded Exhaustive Concordance of the Bible*. Thomas Nelson: Nashville, USA, 2001.

Tate, R. D., Cullis, B. R., Smith, S. D. A., Kelaher, B. P., Brand, C. P., Gallen, C. R., Mandelman, J. W., and Butcher, P. A. "The Acute Physiological Status of White Sharks (Carcharodon Carcharias) Exhibits Minimal Variations After Capture on Smart Drumlines." *Conservation Physiology*, 7 (1) (2019). Accessed February 7, 2022. https://doi.org/10.1093/conphys/coz042

Tyagi, Abhinav, Kumar, Vinod, Kittur, Sagar, Reddy, Mahender, Naidenko, Sergey, Ganswindt Andre, and Umapathy Govindhaswamy. "Physiological Stress Responses of Tigers Due to Anthropogenic Disturbance Especially Tourism in Two Central Indian Tiger Reserves." *Conservation Physiology 7* (1) (2019). Accessed February 7, 2022. https://doi.org/10.1093/conphys/coz045

University of Rochester Medical Center. "Common Injuries of the Shoulder." *Health Encyclopedia* (2022). Accessed February 3, 2022. https://www.urmc.rochester.edu/encyclopedia/content.aspx?contenttypeid=1&contentid=832

Bibliography

University of Rochester Medical Center. "Basic Anatomy of the Heart." *Health Encyclopedia* (2022). Accessed February 4, 2022. https://www.urmc.rochester.edu/encyclopedia/content.aspx?contenttypeid=85&contentid=P00192

Viau, Priscila, Rodini, Debora Cattaruzzi, Sobral, Gisela, Martins, Gabriela Siqueira, Morato, Ronaldo Goncalves, and Alvarenga de Oliveira, Claudio. "Puberty and Oestral Cycle Length in Captive Female Jaguars Panthera Onca." *Conservation Physiology 8* (1) (2020). Accessed February 7, 2022. https://doi.org/10.1093/conphys/coaa052

Webster, Merriam. *Dream* (2022). Accessed January 31, 2022. https://www.merriam-webster.com/dictionary/dream

Yoon, Jungwon, Kim, Gabsoon, Handharu, Nandha, and Ozer, Abdulla. "A Bio-Robotic Toe and Foot and Heel Models of Biped Robot for More Natural Walking: Foot Mechanism and Gait Pattern." *Biped Robots* (2011). Accessed February 4, 2022. http://doi.10.5772/14959

OTHER BOOKS BY THE AUTHOR

Kill That Dog: Deliverance from the Dog Spirit

UPCOMING BOOKS

Strategic Prayers: How to Wage Wars and Win

ENROLL IN OUR POWER-PACKED ONLINE COURSES:

Dream Interpretation 101

Strategic Prayer Skills (1 & 2)

Effective Counselling Skills (1 & 2)

Homiletics

Unlocking the Dream

(Effective Sermon Preparation & Delivery) (1 & 2)

Spiritual Gifts: Discovery and Function

Financial Power & Wealth Sustainability

Self-Esteem Builder & Booster

Masterclass series

TO ENROLL IN OUR EMPOWERMENT COURSES:

Email: slyrankine@yahoo.com

sylvesterrank@gmail.com

Or visit us online at sylvesterrankine.ca

FOR ONLINE COUNSELLING SESSIONS

Email: slyrankine@yahoo.com

SHARE THE MOMENT:

Instagram: sylvester.rankine

Facebook: Apostle Sylvester Rankine

YouTube: Sylvester Rankine

CONTACT INFORMATION:

If you were blessed by this book and would like to contact the author, please send an email to:

Email: slyrankine@yahoo.com

Website: www.citadelchurches.com

www.sylvesterrankine.ca